ON SPECIAL ASSIGNMENT
A STORY OF MISSION

Dr. Bob Bedford

Copyright ©by Robert Bedford 2017

All rights reserved. No part of this publication may be reproduced, stored in a retrieval system or transmitted in any form or by any means, electronically, mechanical, photocopy, recording or otherwise without the prior written permission of the publishers.

Published by Bedford Press, Seminole FL

ISBN: 978-0-9848117-2-4

Printed in the United States

DEDICATION

The story in this book would not have been possible without the constant support and encouragement of my wife, Linda. One of the ways she demonstrated that was her frequent visits to the Atlanta facility. We lived 500 miles to the south. Linda drove that regularly, often by herself.

God sustained her and the van during all that time. There were many times when she would encounter bad weather, and would invite others to join her in praying for safe passage. More than once she saw the "parting of the clouds" with storms on both sides of Interstate 75, but she was driving on "dry ground."

She made that trip to visit 57 times in the 34 months that I was there. There were families who lived locally for the other inmates who did not receive as many visits. Those visits were interspersed with all her other responsibilities as mother, grandmother, and great-grandmother. She also had 95% of the load of the tax business—I contributed what I could.

She also was the communications director, sending out the almost daily emails to keep others informed of the process. In the midst of the ordeal, she fractured her pelvis which required a five-month rehab. Our daughters stood by her during this difficult time.

She made sure that I was provided with commissary money because often that was my lifeline to get nutrition, stamps, and other needed items.

She interacted with the other men in the Visitor's Room, and quickly became a favorite because of her ability to cheer others. If even for a few minutes, their mind was off their circumstances and focused on enjoying the best of the moment.

She was also an active participant with other inmate families. She ministered to them in incredible ways while she was standing in line to be admitted to the visitor's room, interacting with many during the visitation days, as well as responding to them whenever she could to give advice, perspective, and encouragement, not to mention prayer. Several contacted her directly and she was always able to help.

When asked how all of this was possible, she could not give an answer other than it was extraordinary grace that God supplied.

There wasn't enough time to get it all accomplished, but it was. It is simply a story of God's amazing power and a person who allowed God's grace to flow through her to accomplish a most difficult assignment.

For these and a 1000 other reasons, she is to be honored in this story.

Another honorable mention:

One of my dear friends is Pastor Rollin Mitchell. He was just a young teen when I first met him, and he attended the youth camp in Camby, IN, when I was its director. He served as an evangelist during my Atlanta time. He sent a postcard from wherever he was serving almost every week that I was at the camp. Faithful friends such as he cannot be praised enough. He faithfully followed Hebrews 13:3 and I am grateful.

TABLE OF CONTENTS

Recommendations

Chapter 1: PREPARING FOR THE ASSIGNMENT
My Abridged Story

Chapter 2: ACCEPTING THE SPECIAL ASSIGNMENT

Chapter 3: THE FIRST 24 HOURS

Chapter 4: ENTERING THE CAMP

Chapter 5: GODS INTERJECTION

Chapter 6: EARLY CHALLENGES

Chapter 7: THE DAILY GRIND

Chapter 8: PIZZA EVANGELISM

Chapter 9: 2008

Chapter 10: WHEN COMPLICATIONS BECAME A MAJOR FACTOR

Chapter 11: MEDICAL STORY OF ROTATOR CUFF SURGERY

Chapter 12: MEDICAL STORY OF HEART SURGERY

Chapter 13: THE BY-PASS SURGERY STORY

Chapter 14: BACK AT THE FACILITY

Chapter 15: THE JOHNNY STORY

Chapter 16: INDIVIDUAL STORIES

Chapter 17: LINDA'S THANKSGIVING MESSAGE IN 2008

Chapter 18: GOD'S CHARACTER SCHOOL—LIFE LESSONS TAUGHT

EPILOGUE

RECOMMENDATIONS

"I highly recommend you read this exciting book even though at times Dr. Bedford's journey will lead you the reader through some sad and difficult moments. It was intriguing to me to get a behind the scene look at how our prison system works. Get a cup of coffee or your favorite drink and enjoy reading how God's grace shows up in Pastor Bob's life in prison. Also, read about God's intervention in the hard road that his wife Linda had as well for the 1029 days they were separated as he served his time away. The Thanksgiving letter Linda wrote in 2008 is alone worth the price of the book. What a great attitude she had during one the biggest storms of her life!"

Dr. Mark Eckart
Orleans, IN

"It was my privilege and honor to read the book "On Special Assignment." Thank you for this opportunity.

While reading Bob's story I was reminded of the Bible character Joseph, who was put into prison unjustly. He, however, found favor with his fellow prisoners because he manifested a good spirit. He also found that God was able to give him overcoming grace.

Bob found that God's grace was sufficient when accused falsely, when incarcerated unjustly, and when sacrifice was intensified. He, with God's help, turned unpleasant circumstances into an effective time of witnessing for Jesus Christ. God used him to reach many who had never heard the Gospel message; to encourage those who were also unjustly bound, and to train scores of inmates for ministry both inside the prison and after they were released.

Bob truly exhibited Romans 8:28 even in the times of extreme difficulties.

You will both enjoy the book and experience an awakening to life inside the cell."

John W. Zechman, President
Penn View Bible Institute

"If you like a true story with a happy ending, this book is for you. You'll marvel how God brought Bob and Linda through a few very difficult years. I'm reminded of how God takes care of those who put their trust in him. No matter what God allows in our life, his grace is sufficient to bring us through victoriously."

Linda Davis
Sister to the author

PREPARING FOR THE ASSIGNMENT
My Abridged Story

It is hard sometimes to understand how God prepares us for difficult assignments. I was born into a pastor's home where I attended church beginning with the second Sunday I was alive. It was unthinkable to miss a Sunday and we couldn't feign sickness. In a revival meeting the month after I turned 7, I made the decision to follow Christ.

My life involved school and church. My dad thought it was best to be in church "every time the church doors were open." One year, dad kept a written record of our church attendance. If there was a revival in the area (the denomination did not matter), we were there. Some nights there were gospel sings, old-fashioned "singing schools" and many other types of church meetings. That year we were in church 359 nights. That did not count Sunday mornings, revival mornings, VBS, camp meetings, etc., where there were daytime services. Amazingly, I don't ever remember thinking we were over-churched.

Through various evangelists and other encouragers, I made a commitment to read the entire Bible through in a year. That began when I was twelve years old. It has been one of the defining disciplines of my life. I'm writing this the year I will turn 71 years old, and that is a commitment that I have kept.

On Sunday, December 25, 1960, as I was praying in the woods behind the Chickasaw Free Methodist Church, I felt the call of God to preach the gospel. That call brought an immediate positive response in my heart, and I have never doubted that call.

When I finished high school, I immediately enrolled into a Bible college even though I had received a four-year scholarship to the University of Nebraska to study accounting. I applied myself diligently carrying 20 or more semester hours, even while working 40 hours a week in the factory.

A bit of irony occurred during those years. As a result of double-tithing, I was audited by the IRS for the first time when I was a mere 18 years old. I was audited again the next year, and audited again when I was 20. By then I was already student pastoring, so I had to learn the basic rules for ministerial taxes. While I did not initially see these challenges by the IRS as anything other than an aberration in "real life," that next year I desired to get out of the foundry where

On Special Assignment

I had worked for three years. I saw where there was an opening to work for H&R Block, a new company that had just come to the Quad Cities area. After speaking with the area director, and acing their tax knowledge test, I was hired immediately as a local manager where I oversaw eight other tax preparers. I came to understand that this, too, was a calling from God so that I could assist ministers in their need for competent tax service.

Since I saw the tax work as an additional assignment from God, I determined to become the best that I could. I took an additional 90 hours of accounting and tax study. I sat for the Enrolled Agent exam and passed that, giving me authority to represent clients anywhere in the country at every level of the IRS. I later studied and passed the Tax Court Bar Exam (the most difficult professional exam in America) on the first try. I was admitted to practice in 1991 and served dozens of clients over many years. I have now completed my 50th year in tax consulting with over 50,000 tax returns filed.

I served as youth minister to my father during my teen-age years. I taught the adult Sunday School class when I was fifteen. I shared the pulpit with dad. When I left for Bible college in 1964, I kept the focus. I was available for weekend meetings and often traveled to fulfill those assignments. Sleep was often neglected in order to reach my early self-imposed goals.

When Linda and I graduated from college, we accepted a short term assignment to work with Barberton Rescue Mission. I had previously held a crusade there and the lessons learned there have been helpful throughout my ministry years.

We moved on to a pastorate in New Castle PA where we began our family. We adopted our oldest daughter, a bi-racial girl, who was brought to us by the local welfare office based on our experience as foster parents. Ten months later our next daughter was born. During our time there, we saw explosive growth from 25 to 90 in attendance in less than 2 years. Even though we have been gone for over 40 years, the friendships developed are still firm and I'm still "Pastor Bob" to many.

Our next move was to Indianapolis where we saw God moving in our work there. We saw the bus ministry grow the church from 150 in morning worship to 350 in just one year. One of the seven-year old girls who was won to the Lord via the bus ministry has now been a pastor's wife for over twenty years.

Our last pastorate was in St Petersburg FL. The church was in distress having declined by 50% and finances were devastated. Our going there was divinely orchestrated and God moved miraculously. The complete story is told in another publication. After three years, I was elected as a regional superintendent overseeing the churches in a nine-state area as well as the Caribbean. That time, too, was marked by incredible advances in church plants, attendance and membership, as well as monies raised (the traditional measurements by a denomination.)

The purpose in relating these milestones is to show that my life has been focused. There were no "wasted years" as song writers have referenced. Yet in spite of my living out my callings, I came under attack by Satan. I'm sure it was no surprise to God. Neither was God surprised at the difficulties that many Bible characters endured. I have taken great comfort after reading again the stories of Joseph, Daniel, many of the prophets, and then Jesus and the apostles.

In my case, trouble began with the government pursuit of certain clients that I had served for a short while. I had been a tax consultant for 30 years and had recently gained access to a group of businessmen who were members of an organization based out of Denver Colorado. I was invited to speak at a business conference in 1996 and then again in 1997. The primary purpose of inviting me to their annual meeting was to make sure the members were informed as to compliance with all tax laws and rules. Unbeknown to me the IRS had targeted certain members of the organization and they had made a deal with the IRS. The deal involved turning states evidence against the leaders of this business organization.

For the next five years the IRS was actively pursuing several members of this business organization. Just before the statute of limitations would run out the IRS decided to indict the leaders of this business organization and along with them I was indicted on the charge of conspiracy. Those indictments were handed down in November 2002. That was a unique experience as well. Federal marshals did not come and arrest me. I was called on the phone from Tampa saying they had received the indictment and would I

On Special Assignment

mind if they would just mailed it to me. That was fine with me, and so a couple days later it came in the mail.

There was a notice to go to Denver to respond to the summons. I busily set about retaining counsel. I was fortunate to get some recommendations and so flew out to Denver and interviewed an attorney who agreed to take my case. I had a little cash reserve and that served as sufficient to retain counsel. What I discovered later was that there were almost no attorneys who understood tax law enough to challenge all the areas that should have been.

The next day I reported to the Federal Court House in downtown Denver to respond to the indictment. Another irony occurred that day as the procedure was to get fingerprinted and photographed at the court house prior to the hearing. Neither function would work, so they just postponed it to be done another day. However, when the sentencing was complete in June 2007, those functions had never been done.

There were many delays as the Department of Justice was putting together their case. The legal preparations began to consume large amounts of time as various records were examined and responses began to develop. Since my schedule was already completely full, this was an added stress that later took a great toll on me.

At the time of the indictment, I was serving as a Regional Superintendent for the Free Methodist Church. In 1998 I had been elected to serve the nine southeastern states and the Caribbean. After three years I was able to reduce my territory by four states leaving only Louisiana, Mississippi, Alabama, Georgia, Florida, as well as the Caribbean. To serve that much territory required me to fly about 9,000 miles monthly as well as drive about 1,000. Just the travel was time consuming, not to mention that I had to oversee the administration of about 100 churches and the pastoral staffs.

Simultaneously, Linda and I were still serving hundreds of pastors and small businesses with the tax consulting. Linda had already assumed a large portion of the work, but I still had some functions that were unavoidable for me. Particularly during the tax season (February through April) I was working at least 100 hours a week. So preparing a legal defense in the midst of that was exhausting.

In conversations with federal prosecutors, I believed that they were going to drop the accusations against me. In an effort to bolster their case, they examined tax returns that I had prepared for the prior ten years—over 5,000 of them. They could not find a single return they could label as having some falsity. In spite of that, they refused to drop the case. While we cannot prove it, it appeared that if the case was dropped against me, I could have appeared as an expert witness for the other two. That was too big a risk since my knowledge and articulation of the issues would have had huge risk for the prosecutors. So the conspiracy indictment remained. For the next couple years, there were pre-trial hearings and other legal wrangling that added time and stress to my very busy schedule.

The trial began in February 2005. The trial lasted five weeks for the prosecution to present their case. The case was so weak and confused that the panel of defense attorneys decided not to put on any defense and so the case went to the jury. The various details of the trial are scheduled for another book so I will not detail much in this one.

The jury was very thorough in their process and took five weeks in order to return their verdicts. At one point in time during the deliberations, the jury sent a question to the judge regarding tax law. The judge assembled the various attorneys and presented it to them. There was no agreement on the interpretation, so the judge sent back that they had no answer and to make the decision without that answer.

It is very difficult to describe the agony of simply waiting every day for a verdict, and each day to end with no verdict. The lead man had been charged with 24 counts and was convicted on four. His assistant had been charged with 20 counts and was convicted on two. I had been charged with just the one count (conspiracy) and the jury was deadlocked on a verdict.

In November 2006 I was retried on that single count. There were many violations of my constitutional rights and it became apparent to me that the district attorney and the judge were both very corrupt. Details of that will be the subject of another book. Nevertheless, after a day of deliberation the jury returned a verdict of guilty. Sentencing was originally set for mid-March, but my attorney requested it be reset for the end of April in order that I could finish another tax season. That in itself was an irony since the conspiracy charge was connected with tax consulting.

The sentencing hearing was set for April 27, 2007. The government was so ill prepared that the sentencing could not be completed that day. So the judge gave them additional weeks and reset the sentencing date for June 1. The length of a sentence is partially based on "loss to the government." Since they had not proven a single return in which there was a certified loss, they had no basis. Even on that date there were very few answers, so the judge simply made up some numbers so that he could have something to base the sentence he'd already decided to give. The sentence was 42 months and I was given six weeks to self-report. Based on the 15% reduction for good behavior, it meant that I would be spending 30-31 month in a federal facility. I actually spent 34 months due to medical issues at the end of the time.

On July 16, 2007, I reported to the federal prison camp in Atlanta, Georgia. That was the beginning of a journey that lasted 34 months. In this book I will attempt to show that God was at work much before that reporting date. Personally, my challenge was accepting God's grace through such a travesty of justice. Another big challenge was helping my wife to prepare for those months for which I would not be at home. We also prepared the children and grandchildren for all of the unknowns that it meant for them. Then we had our huge circle of church connections as well as our sizable base of tax clients.

It was with significant prayer that we felt that God impressed us to live out this time of our life in the public arena. So all of the news as best we could explain it was published for all of these people to read and even ask questions if they so desired. With that in mind, Linda began a database for all of those interested to receive information as it was happening during this entire process and regularly sent out devotional and info to all those who had requested it.

Since God had allowed this result in spite of the facts and the huge volume of prayer that had ascended on my behalf, we accepted the reality of my being incarcerated. Even as I was preparing mentally for this time, I became aware that God can use all kinds of circumstances for his glory even when it means humiliation personally. So even before I reported to the prison camp, I fully believed that this time would be used of God as "a special assignment" from Him.

ACCEPTING THE SPECIAL ASSIGNMENT

It is never easy to go through a difficult assignment. Sometimes we must go through these trying times in order to draw closer to God. When everything gets stripped away from us except God, we find that he is enough.

To make a mental adjustment that you will be confined is quite the process. Knowing that you are there unjustly makes it humanly twice as tough. But I had several years to learn to trust God in ever increasing levels. I certainly had many kinds of circumstances that God used to teach me trust. But this was unlike any prior experience.

The time had come to report, so on Sunday, July 15, my wife, oldest and youngest daughters, and my friends, Jim and Elaine Dressback, made the drive to Atlanta. We planned to stay with Linda's brother (Tim) overnight, before the "reporting" on July 16 by noon. Tim and his wife, Susan, invited several friends over that Sunday evening as an encouragement. There was visiting and prayer. I'm grateful for those who would pray that night and continue on into the months ahead.

The Dressbacks and our crew met at Cracker Barrel for brunch. This would be the last great meal I would have for many months. Then we made our way to the Prison Camp there in Atlanta. We arrived there about 11:30a. They did not know that I was coming. They were able to find my name in the computer, but the "paperwork" had not arrived, so they had no ability to process me in.

The camp director engaged us in conversation trying to figure out which of us was reporting. When I was identified, he told my wife that she would be doing the time, instead of me. The challenges she would face would be much greater than mine. He told her that the camp was basically "adult day care."

THE FIRST 24 HOURS

The family and friends left about 12:15p and two of us were transported across the property to the adjacent facility. It took 15 minutes for someone to come and let us in. Then the processing began. We had to show everything on our person. We were "patted down" and they found nothing but a ball point pen and my contact lens case. We then entered through a series of locked gates into the Receiving and Discharge area.

We were put into a holding cell. After 30 minutes we were brought some forms to fill out and sign—including permission to get medical information. After another 30 minutes or so a Physician's Assistant showed up for the mental health evaluation. That took about 2-3 minutes and we went back to the holding cell. After pacing for an hour, I was asked if we wanted lunch. My "yes" response got us a couple of sack lunches consisting of a slice of bologna between two pieces of white bread and a slice of cheese. We also received an apple.

We waited from 2:30p to 5p before we were taken for photos. Around 3:30p, an officer came and asked us what we wanted to do with our clothes. I chose to have them sent back to my home. We were led to the clothing room and told to strip, place shoes, clothes, driver's license, etc. in to box. We were outfitted with a faded t-shirt, tan pants, mismatched socks and flat slippers, and then returned to the cell to wait again.

Around 5p we were told that we would be seen shortly to complete the processing. A lady interviewed us for about 2 minutes each, and we returned to the holding cell. Sometime between 6:30p and 7p we were told we would be spending time there in the Transfer Center before being transferred to the camp. Others complained that we had not had dinner so the guard gave us another sack containing the same bologna sandwich, cheese, and an apple.

I was instructed to go to Cell 256 and wait. When I went there and peeked into it, there were 2 beds and both were occupied. I returned to the office thinking there had been a mistake. He told me to return to 256 and wait there. Shortly he came and opened the cell door, and I stepped in. They brought a mat and placed it on the floor. That was to be my "bed" till I went back to the camp. The door was then locked.

On Special Assignment

I introduced myself to Mike and the Hispanic from Ecuador who spoke little English. The cell was small and adding the mat took over 50% of the available floor space. I sat on the mat and ate the bologna and cheese, and then finished off the apple.

Mike offered me a book to read—a novel with crude language and a weird plot. With no other choice of something to read, I continued reading. I engaged in conversation with Mike from time to time and learned some things about the prison system. Atlanta is the transfer hub—people come from all over and then are sent to prisons all over the US. There is another transfer unit in Oklahoma City.

The immediate reason for the overcrowding was that 50 prisoners were to be flown out that day, but after getting to the airport the Bureau of Prison's private plane had mechanical problems so they were returned to this facility. There were several busloads of prisoners who arrived anyway. So three people were assigned to each two-man cell.

Since the holding cells are concrete and steel, the noise and chatter echoes throughout the building. At times, the noise was deafening. It lessened somewhat after lights went out around 10p. My head was near the door and on the floor so the noise prevented me from getting much sleep. I did my exercises, prayed and somehow was able to drift off to sleep.

Sometime in the morning (between 6 and 7a) the cell door was unlocked. That was a signal for us to go get our breakfast. We walked past other cells, down the stairs, picked up our tray and climbed another stairway and back to the cell. We were locked in the cell but the lights were not turned on, so we ate in the dark.

Breakfast consisted of oatmeal (no butter, sugar, cinnamon, etc.), cocoa puffs and a piece of chocolate cake. I mixed the cocoa puffs with the oatmeal and got it down. The cake was surprisingly good. When we finished, we shoved our trays under the door and continued to wait—me on my floor mat. Probably around 8a, the lights were turned on. Mike had a Gideon Bible available and so I did my daily reading.

In further conversation with Mike, I was informed that this facility was a 23- hour lockdown place. Everyone was locked in their cells for 23 hours daily and allowed out for one hour of exercise. That hour did not count the daily walks to pick up the meal trays. He further informed me that it was not unusual for a person to spend one to four weeks in this facility before getting processed into the camp. It is hard to describe the feeling I was experiencing at the prospect of any time in such horrible conditions.

I continue reading the book that Mike loaned me until I heard the door unlocked for the one hour of exercise. Mike gave me the tour around the cells. We stopped at the supply room where I received the personal hygiene kit. Prior to that, I had nothing—not even a towel. The kit included shampoo, toothbrush and paste, a comb, a razor and shaving cream. They also provided a towel and change of underwear.

We continued the tour of the area where a few offices were located for counselors, but they were empty. We ended at the law library and I chose to spend the rest of the time there.

The announcement to return to the cell interrupted my thoughts. I made my way upstairs and was locked in the room. In about 30 minutes, the door was unlocked and a guard called my name. He said we need to go for a medical exam. There were five who needed them and so were taken back to that area. I received a TB test, was examined by a dentist, and then by a medical doctor. They were information gathering times, but it allowed me out of the cell for about 2 hours.

When I realized the deplorable conditions in the locked cells, I prayed that God would show himself still working and that he would rescue me quickly. I asked for Tuesday deliverance. It's hard to describe my gratefulness when God chose to answer that prayer!

Near the end of medical exams, the guard reappeared and called my name along with two others and said we would be transferred to the camp shortly. I quickly discovered that all words have a new meaning in this context. Since the medical time had gone long, we were past the meal time. But the office had asked them to save us a tray and they did. We ate our meals, retrieved our meager items and were transferred back to the Receiving and Discharge area. We were moved several times while we waited for the transportation. Finally, an officer arrived and she drove us to the camp.

ENTERING THE CAMP

When we entered the camp reception office, there was another stack of papers to fill out. Who did we want on our visitor list, phone list, more medical info, etc. Another interview with mostly irrelevant questions and then we were ready for the dorm assignment.

There were eight dorms, each built to accommodate 50-72 people in two-man cubicles. Each one is approximately 9x12 furnished with a bunk bed, two lockers 2x3x1.5', and two folding chairs. Because of overcrowding, many cubicles had 3 or 4 men. The walls between the cubicles are about 5' high. There were 36 cubicles in my dorm, with a huge shower room, a TV room, and a small kitchen with a microwave. There were no locks on the dorms, inside or out. We were free to roam the acreage there.

With all the paperwork finished, I had another interview with an officer on duty that day. He handed me off to another officer to take me to my dorm assignment, each dorm designated by a letter from A to H. I was originally told it would be E25, but when we arrived there was no empty bed. The office looked for an empty bed and located one in a 3-bed cubicle with a top bunk. But before the made that my assignment, they told me to wait. Whether it was my prayer or not, they took me to E32. I was given the bottom bunk and introduced to my roommate, James Armstrong. I was to learn later that he had been moved to the cubicle and assigned the bottom bunk only 20 minutes earlier. He had waited 1.5 years to get a bottom bunk only to give it up to me. (I wouldn't want to admit it, but getting the bottom bunk was probably due to our age difference of over 20 years.)

We were taken to the "laundry" where we were issued four sets of clothing. Most of it at least came close to fitting. The shirt and pants were green. The challenge came in the shoes. In order to get the right length, I needed at least an 11, but the only width they had was 4E. I wear a 2A so I was swimming in them and they killed my ankles if I walked more than a few steps. On the next day, I was able to get some insoles but it only helped a little.

The eating schedule is an early one. Breakfast was served from six to seven, lunch from 10:30 – 11:30a, and supper from 4:15-5:15p. They never ran late on the meals. All food service was handled by the inmates. While the variety was limited and it was definitely "institutional," the quantity was generous. It was "starch heavy" and that's one reason why a lot of fellows gain weight while confined.

There were variations in the menu on a daily basis. There was almost always fresh fruit for breakfast, and salad bars for lunch and supper. By befriending the kitchen crew, one can get little extras. But the clean-up crew wanted everyone to eat fast so they could get their work done and out of there. Since I am a slow eater, I sometimes got stared at and once was told "You're the last one and we're waiting to clean your table."

My cubicle-mate asked me right away if I was a Christian. When I said yes, he told me that a group would meet each Tuesday night and if I went I would also get a care package: flip flops for the shower, toothpaste and a brush, deodorant, etc. I went and was given my package.

The dorms were well air-conditioned and the first night was difficult sleeping because I was very cold. The next day I got a second blanket by going to the laundry at 6:30a. Later that day I was able to obtain a sweat suit which I wore at night to be a little warmer. The thermostat was set at 64 degrees, but it was 16' in the air, meaning that near the floor it was in the 50's.

Notices were posted each morning for anyone who had a "call out." Call outs were for special meetings, medical exams, or conferences. I was on the list the first day for the medical office. I reported on time and waited for 20 minutes, only to be told that the papers I had previously filled out were sufficient and to go back to my dorm.

GOD'S INTERJECTION

Released to wander the grounds, I began to explore. I walked up near the chapel, and a gentleman stopped me. "Can I ask you a question?" I nodded that was okay. "Are you a minister?" he asked. I responded, "Why do you ask?" He stated, "There was just something about your spirit that made me wonder." I acknowledged that I was. He then indicated that he was delighted and wanted to develop a friendship. (That friendship has lasted long past the Atlanta experience.) I learned that he too had ministerial experience. His crime was that he had received prescription medicine for pain. When he became well enough that he no longer needed the medicine, he sold what was left. He was not aware that was illegal. While he survived the poor medical help of the prison system, he is now in hospice care and awaits his home-going to heaven. See further notes below on Larry Roundtree.

About 30 minutes later, another gentleman approached me with the same question, "Are you a minister?" Again, I wanted to know why he was asking. He responded that he had been praying that God would allow a minister to come here so that he could be discipled and taught the scriptures. When I indicated that I was, he asked if I would be willing to teach him the Bible while we were both in Atlanta. I agreed, and thus began a mentoring situation which continued throughout my time of incarceration.

Those two confirmations were significant to me that God was going to use my time in Atlanta for the good of the kingdom. Having others come almost every week allowed God to continually affirm in my heart that He had not forsaken me, and would empower me with his grace to accept this difficult assignment.

God met other needs as well. Less than one week into my confinement, God provided a watch for me, as well as a pair of tennis shoes that were the right size (no easy task!) A note in the journal for July 23, 2007 stated, "God continues to answer prayers for lots of little things. Opportunities to minister present themselves several times per day. Someday we'll fully understand this." I remember God speaking to me and reminding me that he had called me to lead and train men into reproducing disciples. He added that just because my venue had changed, my assignment had not!

EARLY CHALLENGES

While God was at work in very definable ways, there were daily challenges. Some additional thoughts from the journal:

Incompetence, indifference, and ineffectiveness are all terms that can be applied to the Bureau of Prisons. In a world of moral confusion, the BOP has no idea what their mission is. So a system has been created where there are different levels of control. The term penitentiary is applied to maximum security facilities and there is one "super-max" in Florence Colorado, which is underground and inmate rarely see the light of day. In the medium to low security category, they are known as Federal Correctional facilities.

The programming that exists is limited to helping inmates get a GED, some low-level vocational education, or drug rehab classes. Staff members, by and large, are recruited from lower walks of life, who see it as a job. The inmates' welfare is of little consideration.

In the minimum-security level, the facilities are designated as "camps" and inmates live in dormitories. Generally, there are no fences or gates. While official counts are taken several times a day, you are free to do as you please on the property. Everyone is supposed to have a "job" and you are paid. Wages range from 12 cents per hour to 40 cents. The average worker might get 20 hours a week.

To my knowledge, there were no attempts to address the issues that were responsible for putting people into incarceration. While they give an anemic psychological evaluation, unless you demand treatment, you will get none. If you do demand it, it usually amounts to giving prescription drugs.

They had three chaplains on staff but that was for all three facilities on the property. There were about 500 men at the camp, about 2500 in the adjacent medium security facility, and around 500 passing through the Transfer Facility. The needs in the medium security facility were more pressing so over 90% of the time, they were there.

In the camp, there were case managers and counselors. Each inmate was assigned to one of each. After two weeks, I had met with the counselor for two minutes, and I had yet to meet the case manager.

On Special Assignment

About a month before I entered the camp, I was diagnosed with diabetes. The doctors are quite sure it was the result of stress since my lifestyle is quite healthy. Anyone who knows me can verify that I don't have a weight problem. I exercise regularly. My eating is certainly in a healthy mode.

As an example of the inefficiency that prevailed: I was to get my sugar checked three times a week. It was scheduled at 6:30a since it should be done before one eats. However, the doctor did not show up until 6:50a. By the time the test was taken, the meal line had been closed. I think that would be called "forced fasting." But I survived.

There are many items labeled "contraband." Among the items are cigarettes and cell phones. Everyone was well aware the place was flooded with both. The mantra was "just don't get caught." The unit manager told me that he believed there were around 300 cell phones in a population of 500.

Standard procedure requires that each new arrival be given a battery of medical tests within the first two weeks. After four weeks, none of that had happened. Had I not forced the issue by reporting to sick call and simply waiting several hours, it may never have happened. Based on my sugar levels around 400, I knew it was medically necessary to get some treatment.

I reported earlier about the problem with shoe sizes. The ones issued to me were seven sizes too wide, and created multiple problems trying to wear them. Supposedly, shoes were to be ordered to fit, but during the 34 months that had never happened. I was able to get a medical pass that allowed me to wear tennis shoes, so I again found a way to cope.

The TV room had four TV sets. In order to hear, you had to obtain a headset which could be dialed to the set you wanted to watch. Many spent most every waking hour there. I had no interest. My sole time to watch was about ten minutes when my oldest granddaughter was featured on American Idol.

The head orderly would gladly do your laundry. There are two washers and dryers in each unit. If you can find one not in use, you are fortunate. If you hire the orderly, everything is neatly folded

Bob Bedford

and laced on your bed. Everything comes with a price. The price was "two macs."

It becomes necessary to understand the "in prison" currency. Since cash is forbidden, an alternative currency was essential. Other facilities may have used postage stamps, or another commodity, but this was based on a 100g package of mackerel—an edible bag of fish which could be obtained at the commissary for $1.20. The black market at this camp was all based on the "mac." I was told that a "mac" could be passed around for 2-3 years before being finally eaten. Those that provided "services" to other inmate could accumulate hundreds of these "macs."

Haircuts were free (one of the jobs assigned in the camp was barber) but if you wanted a good haircut, the inmate barber wanted a tip of three macs!

Life in the camp all revolved around the "counts." The most important one seemed to be the 4 o'clock stand up count. Everyone reported to their cubicle and stood there when the officer arrived to physically count everyone. Should someone be missing, everyone was confined until they could determine who was missing. At this particular camp they had also started an 8p count as well as the standard 10p count.

Between the close of supper around 5p and the 8p count, there was a variety of things to do. There was a ¼ miles track to walk. That area also had a basketball court, racquetball court, volleyball courts and a baseball field. There was a sizable covered area that had machines: treadmill, bikes, weights, etc. There was also shuffleboard, bocchi ball, and tables to play games. Ping pong, air hockey and pool tables were available. There were a leather craft shop and a leisure library that had some 2000 books.

There certainly was a change of reading habits. While I am an avid reader (averaging a book a week), most of my reading is religious or business. I forced myself to read at least one novel a year. But with so much time on my hands, I read about 200 novels during my time there—more than all the novels I had read in my first 60 years!

The camp population was about 60% black, 10% Hispanic, and a few Asians. I was there for several months before I met an unkind person. I was introduced to a number of attorneys and they helped me with my legal research. Also, there were doctors, ministers, and many businessmen.

I was there about 10 days before they finally had "orientation" for all the newcomers. It was held in a large room with poor acoustics so I could barely understand anything that was being said. The material was very general in nature so I counted that a "wasted day." What I needed to know was learned from talking to the other inmates.

One of the other ministers who was there decided to create a new program which he called "The PATH." (PATH stood for Purpose Achieved Through Him.) The program was a teaching/mentoring program designed to help inmates find a new future once they were out. The mentors were determined to make the best of their time there and serve God faithfully.

The PATH program continued to provide basic teaching on many practical items. We would often up to sixty men in the sessions. Well over half the men had never had a checking account, much less understanding how to balance the account.

One of the issues that we faced often (and it is prevalent across our American culture) was that few had truly been discipled. Many thought the answer to that was good Bible study. However, I taught them that we needed Bible application more than knowledge. We needed to raise the level of obedience to their level of knowledge. That changed the focus of many of our groups, and accountability to do what the Scripture instructed was of vital importance.

I haven't said much about my roommate yet. His name was James and he was just a couple years older than my oldest daughter. James has a Christian mother and was reared with that knowledge. He was in there on a drug charge but he had not been a drug user. He had received a 20-year sentence and had worked his time down so that he could be housed at a camp. The regulations state that a person cannot be assigned to a camp (minimum security) until they have 10 years or less on their sentence.

He had some unusual habits such as sleeping during the day and staying awake all night. He was a very calm person, and had many occasions to make my life more comfortable. It was extremely unusual that one gets to keep a roommate long term—but he was the only one I had during the entire term

James became my primary protector, mentor, and confidante on all prison matters. I will explain much more as time goes on, but I could always depend on him. After I had been there about a month, James quizzed me thoroughly about why I was there. After explaining the circumstances, he told me that he had suspected that I was simply a "plant" by the Bureau. He said, "You were just too nice to have committed a crime." Nevertheless, I was there and he fully understood the injustice that occurs to many through the corruption of prosecutors and judges.

It was apparent in the early days of my confinement to believe that God would intervene and somehow through some appeal process that I would be released early. As you will come to see, that simply was not the case. Time after time, the judges either ignored the arguments or simply postponed a decision (which in effect denies the request.)

Part of the ministry was to assist other inmates through their disappointments. In my entry on August 20, 2007 I wrote about two of them. Pastor Lee received word that his youngest son was taken to an optometrist and the testing showed very bad eyesight. Only four years old, he would need very thick glasses. My response was to share my story of God's intervention in my eyesight. At age five, and getting an exam for entry into kindergarten, the doctor discovered that I was blind in my left eye, and the vision in the right eye was 20/400. Sitting in the front row of the classroom I could not see the blackboard. The doctor warned that I could be completely blind in five years or so.

Many doctors do not know the great Physician, and even those who do don't always acknowledge his intervention in people's lives. While I was not healed quickly, God began a process of improving eyesight that would continue for over 60 years. Every time I would get my eyes examined, the prescription would be a little less. Also, by the time I was seven, I had regained eyesight in my left eye although it was not perfect.

Fast forward to today, and I no longer wear glasses except for night driving. I don't need reading glasses even at age 70. The last transition to wearing no glasses (or contacts) came while I was in Atlanta. God truly is amazing, and sharing that story with Pastor Lee was of great encouragement.

THE DAILY GRIND

From the time that I was assigned the job with the visitor's center cleaning crew, I worked side by side with Phil Driscoll, the world-famous trumpeter. When I first met him, he was really struggling with his confinement. As I found with many of the men there, there had been a lot of injustice and I'm convinced that Phil had no business being there. But all of us struggle with a deeper question: why didn't God intervene to keep us out of prison? As I shared my story with him, he came to realize that many of us had similar stories, and in my case my sentence was over three times what he had received.

Other than coping with the injustice, he had basically confined himself to his cubicle. But I, along with others, encouraged him to use his incredible talents to minister to the ones who were there. I remember the day after the Labor Day weekend as we went to work cleaning the visitor's center. When Phil walked in that day, there was a new shine on his face. His opening words to me were, "Bob, I got my song back last night."

From that day until he left in December, he was a major blessing to all the men there. He began holding "concerts" and presenting the gospel in each of those events. He received permission to do a Christmas concert in the Visitor's Room, attended by many of the guards and officials of the prison. He was able to write an entire album of new songs during that time, which he recorded shortly after his release.

One of my personal challenges with health was diabetes. The blood sugar check had readings in the 300's almost every day. It took over six weeks before the BOP got me an oral medicine—glyburide. I tried to be very selective in what I was eating. I was very faithful in walking the track, usually about four miles a day. In spite of that, my blood sugars stayed about 250. The medicine had brought it down 100 points but it was still excessively high.

On August 29, 2007, my roommate, James, became a grandfather—a seven-pound girl delivered C-section. As is usual with many inmates, it would be months before he was able to see his granddaughter.

On August 31 of that year, I wrote Linda: I woke early (5a) and took a shower, walked a mile, dropped the outgoing mail into the box, checked my sugar (reading of 226), ate breakfast, and read my

On Special Assignment

scripture and devotional all by 7a. I worked for 30 minutes followed by another two-mile walk, and then read till 9a. I then headed to my private office (visitor's room) and wrote a new devotional and answered a letter. I ate a quick lunch (baked fish and salad) and then took a short nap. That was followed by 1.5 hours of racquetball. I cleaned up to go for supper of chili mac (it actually had chili powder this time) and salad with a small piece of carrot cake, and then on to our afternoon Bible study. Then it was back to the dorm for the 4 o'clock stand up count and mail call.

One of the challenges that so many face is that friends and family desert you if you are imprisoned. In Doug's case, Dr. Mike's roommate, it was his pastor who failed to make any contact for over two years, and he was local. It had given occasion to develop considerable bitterness on his part. While God will always provide us with ample grace not to get bitter, it is easy to resist that grace. Witnessing to Doug was very difficult. But in the first part of September, Doug received word that the pastor had requested approval to come visit him. Just that was enough to soften Doug's heart.

So many on the outside ignore the biblical imperative, "Remember the prisoners, <u>as though in prison with them</u>, and those who are ill-treated, since you yourselves also are in the body." (Heb 13:3 NASB, emphasis added)

I noted on September 6th that I had received 17 pieces of mail. Many of those were birthday cards. It was remarkable that my friends and family were so supportive. I received over 1800 pieces of mail in those 34 months from over 400 different people. Many times a particularly encouraging note would be shared with others—especially those who received no mail. It seems the longer someone is confined, the less people on the outside seem to remember. But mail and visits are vital to an inmate's well-being.

One of the challenges that confronted us was the "lock-out." An announcement would come over the loud-speaker system that we were to report to the recreation area and "wait." During that time, the guards would go through the dorms looking for contraband, namely, cigarettes, alcohol, and cell phones. Often it was a game with the inmates. One fellow whose dorm was being searched went to another dorm, borrowed a cell phone, and ordered a replacement phone knowing his would be confiscated. By the next afternoon, he had another cell phone. The trick was to erase any contact numbers so that the phones could not be traced. Often the phones were hidden in unusual places: in the ceiling tiles, in a mattress, in the chapel or music room, and sometimes in the back of a typewriter in the law library.

You might be wondering how could contraband be delivered when everyone was searched coming into the camp. Where there are restrictions, human ingenuity excels. The 12' fence (with barbed wire at the top) around the camp property was a simple barrier. Some of the inmates could scale that, go and pickup any kind of item and be back in their dorm within seven minutes. Often the guys would simply go and get some fast food because they hated the institutional food so much.

Other avenues for contraband delivery was to get it to those who worked outside the fence such as the food warehouse. Many of the guards could be "bought" so they often looked the other way as men would come in through the gate loaded with various items. Sometimes they would know how to position items on the outside of the fence, where there were disguised "holes" and then retrieve the items later when no guard was watching.

It was in those times that I wrote, "I'm quite sure the animals have seized control of the zoo." The upset in schedule would sometimes eliminate me playing racquetball, but I compensated by walking more, as much as six miles in a day.

Another gentleman that I ministered to was named Udo. I asked him his nationality and he told me Nigerian. I told him I had been in Nigeria the previous year and he was very amazed. Then I met Dominic from Ghana, where I had also been that prior year. While both men promised to re-contact me once they were out, I have not heard from either of them. But often, God simply puts someone in our life's path for just a period of time. Making those moments count keeps us focused on God's vision.

There were challenges because of the unique differences between guards. One of those was called "Parsons" and he was known for his gruffness and "being by the book." When he did mail call, he was supposed to verify your identity by having you state your BOP

On Special Assignment

reference number. He would require you to do it for each piece of mail. So if you had three pieces, you gave your number three times. I have the privilege of breaking his routine because of the large amount of mail. It happened the day I received 17 pieces of mail!

Another of the anomalies was occasionally they would have a "census count." By that we reported to our cubicle and had to present our official ID's. No one can figure the timing of these events. From the inmate's standpoint, it is just another worthless interruption. Maybe it makes the guards feel more important that they have an assignment.

While there were many opportunities for prayer, Dr. Ben wanted to establish a specific prayer time with me. We set aside 30 minutes a day where we would address the various needs that had come to us. We would start with quoting a psalm or hymn and then we would alternate every 2-3 minutes with each of us addressing some specific request. That time went by very quickly, but it allowed us to mention specific needs. While we did not keep a "prayer journal" for those sessions, we did see some miraculous answers to prayer.

One evening when Dr. Ben came for prayer time, my roommate inquired about his ability to look at his hurting foot. Ben asked several questions, did a short exam by searching for sore spots. James had sprained his ankle a couple months previously, and it had not come back to normal. Ben had James sit down on the bed and then manipulated his foot. We heard a "snap" and his ankle was re-aligned and the pain was gone. Regardless of the profession that a person had on the "outside," inside we were all on the same plane. But using various skills that each one had, we were all able to serve each other in various ways.

I was trying to increase my visitor's list. (Originally, they gave permission to close family members.) The process involved getting a "visitor's form" from the counselor and then they would vet the proposed visitor before giving them approval. I wanted to add six people but the counselor would only give me two at a time because it would increase his work load. So I would go weekly and get two forms.

Another sad statistic regarding imprisonment is the increasing divorce rate. Typically, marriage will survive about 50% of a sentence. If a wife filed for divorce, there was virtually nothing an inmate could do except accept it. That was the case with Gary. He walked a couple laps with me one morning to share that he was expecting a visit from his wife the next weekend. However, instead of being excited to see her, he had a premonition that she would be telling him she was filing for divorce. Since he still had four more years, he could do nothing to oppose it. His wife had just gotten tired of waiting. We had prayer for God to give him peace and grace.

Another man (Greg) received word that his twenty-one-year-old son had been shot to death the previous day. Naturally, he was overcome with grief, especially at not being able to just be there for other family members. The BOP is generally unresponsive to any request to leave for a couple days to participate in a family gathering. We were able to surround him with prayer and sympathy.

There were always new examples of government nonsense. The previous warden had some unspent funds in a prior year budget so he decided to build a garage to repair the trucks and buses. He spent $3 million to have it built. However, the bus and trucks are all broken down since they have no budget to buy the parts, even if the inmates could do the work. The men assigned to work those details are required to show up for work and be there, but they can't work because there are no parts.

One of the grosser details that men live with was the fact that toilet paper was a rationed item. The allotted supply was more than adequate for me, but others who used a lot, or who had a period of sickness, were at the mercy of their friends. That was something I had never before given any thought.

Because some bureaucrat decided that people get into crime because they lack education, the BOP began a big push to create an educational program to help inmates get their GED. To encourage the various prisons to promote it, they gave an incentive of $2500 for each student who would pass the test. But bureaucrats never seem to think something completely through. The process made each new inmate "prove" they had a high school diploma. It didn't matter that a person could show they had a college degree (or in my case two earned doctorates), only a certified copy of the high

On Special Assignment

school diploma/transcript would suffice. Until that documentation arrived, everyone was required to go to the remedial classes. Fortunately, for me it only took about three weeks for mine to arrive. Can I let you know that the best of the GED teachers were boring?

Track time was a major time of "discipling" for me. I was introduced to another black pastor, this one from Jacksonville who was here on tax issues as well. He walked six laps with me that day so we could talk. He only had a six-month sentence so we had to work quickly. Walking the track was on my daily schedule. It was the best time for those not on my regular schedule to talk. A fellow could get good exercise while opening his heart and mind to scriptural teaching.

I had mentioned earlier that the camp included a music room. I have enjoyed playing the piano since childhood, and often just play for the joy of it. In the camp, it was a great refuge. In the midst of the craziness, I could shut out a lot of noise and engross myself in some of the great hymns such as "Oh Worship the King." Then I would worship while playing many songs like, "Great is Thy Faithfulness" or "It is Well with my Soul." Next, it would move into the great Southern Gospel songs.

Fellow inmates would often come and listen for a while, and even occasionally a guard. Counselor Brye came in, listened for a while, and said, "You play pretty well." I thanked him and he left. Getting a compliment from him plus a smile was really big for him. Then I had a couple guys asked me if I would teach them. One followed through and over a six-month period became a decent player. My basic teaching plus his dogged determination by practicing 2-3 hours each day paid off.

In spite of the fact that I was struggling with diabetes, it was extraordinarily difficult just to get basic medicine. I would run out and have none for sometimes weeks. My sugar counts would go from 180 up to 300. I figured out part of the delay. The government operates on a fiscal year ending September 30 each year. The BOP had used up all their budgeted money for this fiscal year so they put everything off the last days of September and would re-engage on October 1. This was just another example of the gross mismanagement in the system exacerbating the imprisonment of undeserving people.

My days just kept getting more crowded as men would desire mentoring. It is such a shame that no one had stepped up to offer these men that kind of relationship before they were incarcerated. On September 27, 2007 I noted that I spent an hour with Dessie, and he wanted more. So he walked with me for two miles around the track while we talked. Then I spent an hour with Doc, followed by 1.5 hours with Alfredo, and then about 30 minutes with Chico, and finished that afternoon with Lee. It was a very full day, but lives were changing and that made it very worthwhile.

Early in October 2007, the PATH program that I mentioned earlier held its first "graduation." The men had learned various skills as basic as how to balance a checkbook, improving their English grammar, math, and science studies, as well as how to prepare a resume and look for a job. The ceremony began with a 30-minute concert by Phil Driscoll with emphasis on his trumpet. Phil began with some keyboard and singing like his music mentor, Ray Charles, for whom he played for several years. There were a few remarks by the leader, Lee Robbins, and then nice certificates were passed out to the graduates. Even the camp director attended and seemed to enjoy it.

By October 9 (less than three months at the camp) I had emptied four ball point pens with all of my writing: responding to mail (I answered everyone for whom I had an address), writing devotionals, preparing lessons for all the mentorees, and writing the legal research and briefs. Looking back at the letters, I realize that my penmanship needs some upgrading!

It was obvious from the beginning and in all the early months, that while I accepted the fact that I was "on assignment" from God, that I still believed that he would shorten my time. It wasn't just me, but most of the men believed that God would intervene through legislation, revised court decisions, or some other option. But time began to stretch out, and deliverance was no closer.

One observation that became very clear was that the "rules" of the camp deviated from what was written to become whatever the particular guard on duty wanted. One could be stricter than the letter of the law, or he could totally disregard it. Once the men knew a guard, they would adjust their behavior accordingly. Even then the actual behavior could vary greatly from the façade that men displayed under scrutiny. For example, one rule that existed for the dining hall was that you could not take food out of the dining, only eat while you were. But lots of time the guard was paying no attention, and since there were two exits, the men would go to the exit farthest away from the guard. One day, the administrator of the camp was the guard on duty and he was checking to see that food was not being taken out. So I joked with him a little about him doing that. He responded that at least people shouldn't flaunt it which told me he was fine with me slipping a couple cookies in my pocket—just so he couldn't see it.

Linda was so diligent in getting the communication system set up for our friends. It was a monumental effort to type the devotionals that I would send her, plus add her own writings about the experiences. By mid-October she reported that the Philippians 1:12 blog showed that 702 devotionals had been downloaded in September. And in the first eight days of October, another 157 were downloaded. I am convinced that the blogs kept the friends informed and that served as a catalyst for people to pray. Those prayers went a long way in keeping me encouraged and the ministry effective in this difficult place.

By the time I was there three months, I was wishing daily for the experience to end. Even though I was able to be a blessing to many people, they were still all rooting for me to get an early date to go home. My focus, even at that point, was to establish the discipling so deeply that it would live for a long time without me there. It was similar to a missionary approach—you're most successful when you are no longer needed. Throughout the notes, it was apparent that I had hope of being released in the very short term, but we know that for whatever reason God had, that prayer was not answered.

Every day during those first months, I was in the law library helping to research for the sake of assisting the attorney preparing my appeal. Since he was based in Salt Lake City, communication was difficult and not very frequent. The courts were very negligent as well. It took about four months just to get the case files transferred to him. I wrote and sent him details of the case as I understood it. But since he also, like my previous attorneys, had little to no experience doing tax cases. Add to that the slipperiness of a "conspiracy" charge, where there was no underlying charge, and it was like trying to get your hands to hang onto a large greasy blob of fat.

I noted on October 10 that the air conditioning had stopped working in our dorm, and I was rejoicing! They brought in a large fan near the end of the dorm and it circulated the air. But for the first night that I was there, I had a pleasant sleep without being cold.

When I received my work assignment, I was given a higher pay scale. Normally, men start and 12 cents per hour and work their way to as much as forty cents. But when I received my first pay, I was receiving 17 cents an hour. For the month of September, I earned $14.10!

Even after three full months of being at the camp, I still had not had the initial medical checks which were to include a chest x-ray, EKG, and blood work. In spite of my medical history, the incompetence of the BOP could not get it scheduled. My notation at the time was "a broken system run by incompetents equals insanity."

The start of my fourth month had an interesting note. Dr. Mike shared that he and his roommate had received notes from Vivian, our dear friend here in St Petersburg who served on staff at the church. She had responded to my appeal for people to write letters to inmates who received little or no mail. Both men were impressed that someone who did not know them would take the initiative to write a note of encouragement. We had been witnessing to Raymond for weeks, but he was reluctant to trust God because so many had disappointed him in life. But for Raymond this simple act of kindness was incredible. That evening he accepted Christ as his Savior. He requested to be baptized and we were able to do that as well.

We wanted to baptize all new believers, but that was a challenge since there was no baptismal available, and no lakes of water on the premises. But ingenuity goes to work. We were able to secure a large portable container from the laundry room. We moved it to the chapel and filled it with water. We let it sit for a couple days so it could warm up. Then by having the men on their knees in the container we were able to submerge them. Linda sent in "baptismal certificates" so we could give each man a lasting memorial of the

On Special Assignment

sacred event. We had received that supply of blank certificates a few days earlier, so each of those who had been baptized received a nice signed Baptismal Certificate to commemorate that milestone in their life.

Another example of God working in the camp had to do with the chapel. By regulation, the chapels are supposed to be led by a chaplain. There were three paid chaplains in Atlanta but with the population of the medium security prison at 2500, the needs there were primary. Because of the heavy load, the chaplain came and talked to Lee and me, to see if we would take over the Protestant service (contrary to the regulations.) We readily agreed. Lee and I shared the duties until he left in 2009, assigning various ones to do the music, the prayer, and the speaking.

Another gentleman who was a UM pastor from Jacksonville, Charles, talked to me and affirmed my leadership. There was not a day in which there were no men who were seeking spiritual help. With God's help, I was able to draw upon the training and experience to direct them into new depths of understanding. On another day, Charles stopped me and made this statement, "You're not here because of something you did wrong. You're on a divine appointment. You're making a difference here." I'm so amazed at the affirmation that I received from all the men, but especially the black population.

When men became aware of my background in tax issues, I was flooded with requests to review and help their individual cases. Some wanted help with business plans they were constructing for when they were released. My primary motivation was to gain the goodwill that would allow me to minister to them spiritually. That happened time and time again.

My notes reflected that I hoped and sensed that I would get an early release. While that never happened, it was interesting how that hope would keep me encouraged and uplifted a few more weeks. I noted in November that I had survived 4.5 months. "I'm ready for that miracle (of release) no matter how God wants to fashion it." The black pastor, Charles, on December 1 asked me how much time I had and I gave him the dates. He responded that his spirit told him that I would be released within a month. In spite of his certainty, early release was not on the horizon.

Part of the craziness that we were subjected to on a daily basis was emergency counts. On November 30th, I noted that the guards did not do a 10p count. They usually turned the lights out shortly after that count. But at 11p that night, no count had been taken so I went to bed anyway. My roommate, James, told me they never came until they did their usually midnight count with just a flashlight. No explanations were ever given.

By December 1, we were in a severe water restriction time. Even washing clothes could only be done on the weekends. Showers were limited to a maximum of five minutes. But I had made friends with a couple of the laundry guys and they would accommodate me anytime I needed something.

December brought a number of releases: Ken, Jay, Alfredo, and Phil. Their leaving, as with others, brought a time of reflection for me. Was I faithful to minister to their needs, and did I assist them in preparing for the "outside." Those questions could not be quickly answered and had to be left with God. Time would eventually tell.

Raymond was one of those inmates who had no relatives living. He was bitter against God and most of the world. We chose to befriend him as Jesus would have done. Alone in the prison camp, he received no letters or visits. His only income source was his job which paid about $17 a month. When I made known to our friends, they responded by sending enough funds so that I was able to purchase from the commissary the following items: a sweat suit, thermal top and bottom, long sleeve t-shirt, shower slippers, three bottles of vitamins, batteries, a bag of peanuts, and four packs of popcorn. It was a Christmas to remember. It was the first time I saw him be genuinely grateful and he said, "I want to write them and thank them." That was huge progress!

We entered the Christmas season with some great worship of Jesus and emphasis on the advent. It's amazing that in confinement, people can set aside their disappointments and frustrations for a time. Christmas was a joyous time and many came to know the Lord during that time.

PIZZA EVANGELISM

The Christian men in Dorm E got together and decided to pool their resources to put on a pizza party to have opportunity to share the gospel. This did require a lot of creativity. The crust was made from tortillas. They were moistened and then stuck together to fill the pan with the sides rolled up to resemble a typical crust.

Pizza sauce was not available in the commissary so a kitchen worker persuaded the officer in charge to donate enough from the kitchen. He also gave us a block of mozzarella cheese, which was grated on a prison-made grater. The men collected tomatoes, onions, and bell peppers from those who had a vegetable diet. Sharp knives are contraband, so the men have taken tin can lids and bent one side over to act as a handle, creating a sharp dicing machine.

Some meat was available from the commissary: pepperoni, beef and turkey logs which were also diced. Cajun seasoning was also available. Around 6p they started assembling the pizzas and they were all prepared within an hour. Immediately after the 8p count, they assembled to do the cooking. There were two microwaves available in our dorm and they were going full blast for about an hour.

The soft drinks were iced down using the mop bucket lined with a plastic liner so they were ice cold by serving time.

Everyone in the dorm was invited to assemble—about 70 at that time. Around 50 chose to come and Lee welcomed them and explained this was a gift of the Christians in the dorm and we were there to serve them. I gave a short Christmas blessing and Chico prayed a thanksgiving for the food. Each man received several slices of pizza, a can of soda, and wonderful fellowship. They may have only come for the food, but they were shown Christian love. The excitement and gratefulness for the evening was obvious and a whole new level of comradery was begun.

A gospel strategy says we cannot wait for people to seek God. As Jesus demonstrated, it is our responsibility "to seek and to save" those who are lost. (Luke 19:10) Even with severe limitations, we can spread the gospel. That weekend it was with a prison pizza party.

2008

We always greet a new year with lots of hope, and this was no different. It had become increasingly clear that deliverance would not come soon.

Obviously, the pressures on us as a family that came from my confinement were huge. One of those was financial. Even though we had prepared for this possibility, we simply could not anticipate every need. We never felt clear to make any appeal for funds. Some made attempts to assist but many good intentions of some did not materialize. Early in the year, we needed to pay the taxes on our home. We did not share that need, and it was a substantial sum. However, God in his faithfulness laid it on the heart of some dear friends here in Florida. They sent a check for a substantial sum that came within a little bit of paying the entire amount. It was another lesson God was teaching us that we could trust Him! It wasn't just a lesson, but a whole course that God was teaching us on trust.

It was the last week of January, when a new man arrived named Ty Short from Alabama. He had a Master's Degree in theology, and we quickly developed a friendship. Then another man arrived who was a judge from Mississippi. He had been accused of bribes in an obvious political struggle and was there very unjustly as well. The BOP was very negligent in getting him his medicine and as a result he suffered a heart attack. By the grace of God, he survived, but he was taken to a local hospital for care. What a life—two weeks in confinement and the next two weeks in the hospital getting a triple by-pass.

Day after day my time was more than busy. It involved doing my work assignment, spending two hours reading and then writing my devotional for the day. I had teaching/mentoring sessions with Mike, Todd, Ben, Kenny, and then Lee.

It was a daily game for the inmates and the guards to determine who could be the most deceptive about the cell phones. Getting caught with a cell phone was considered an "escape attempt." The punishment included getting shipped to a low security facility, loss of some of the "good time," and sometimes additional time added. A young man, James, was caught with a cell phone just two days after he obtained one.

On Special Assignment

I had been at the camp for six months before the head chaplain came for a Sunday service. She spoke primarily on integrity and she wasn't bashful to name specific sins of this place. One of the ironies is that the guards were generally bigger law breakers than the inmates. But as is often the case, bureaucrats overlook the obvious, and proclaim, "Do as I tell you, not as I do."

One of the challenges we faced with the chapel services was over diversity. With 70% of the inmates here from the African American community, we obviously must have accommodated them. But even so, there was still the disparity between young and old. Some had been reared in the church, and some were brand new to Christianity. Then there was every kind of theological sect, and a variety in preaching styles. Somehow we were able to navigate through all of that, and God's presence was felt, sometimes very deeply. It was further interesting that of all those in "leadership" for the chapel, quite often I was the only white present.

While officially the BOP encourages contact with the outside, particularly family, it is neither convenient or cheap. For example, the phone system is a profit center for some outside contractor. While it could be made to be very cheap through using the internet, the basic cost for a local call was 6 cents per minute. Long distance was 23 cents a minute. Added to that was the allocation of just 300 minutes a month, except November and December when it was increased to 400.

We allocated ten minutes a day so that we could stay in contact. With Linda continuing the tax business, there were often lots of questions for which she needed answers. When the calls were well planned, we got an amazing amount of things accomplished with each phone call. If for some reason the call was interrupted, it was necessary to wait one hour before placing the call again.

Evening time was the major time to make calls, so people would line up to use the phone. There was only one phone per dorm which housed up to 72 inmates. Because there were counts at 8p and 10p, the phone was almost always busy between those hours.

I became aware that there was a currency exchange within the camp. I previously told you about the "mac" (package of mackerel). Many of the men were very enterprising—finding all kinds of ways to earn additional funds. Mike was a currency exchanger. He would "buy" in quantity from other inmates, and then would sell them to his "inner circle" for 80 cents. (They cost $1.30 at the commissary.) Others would pay him by buying what he wanted from the commissary. So since that saved 50 cents per mac, I took advantage of that commerce.

There were always men who sensed their need of things spiritual. Conversions happened in the Bible studies and private meetings in the dorm more than in the chapel services. One such man was Steve, who had been reared Jewish. Doc Mike was very instrumental in bringing him around. We introduced him to the gospels and he read all four in a matter of a week. He was to make a profession of faith, and receive Christian baptism. It was important to him that he not reject his Judaism, but receive Christ as a "completed Jew." He also addressed the issue that he was not good enough to be accepted by Christ. We explained that God accepted us based on the atoning work of Jesus, and that accepting God's grace would begin the transformation within him. Doc Woodward was very involved in planning the baptismal service. We also enjoyed the enthusiasm that Steve showed in the Bible studies.

The day came for Steve's baptism. He faithfully answered the questions in our ritual. One of the questions was, "Steven, do you believe that Jesus Christ died for your sins, that this atonement is the only means of Salvation, and that He rose again to give you life eternal?" It was marvelous to hear him respond, "This I also believe." It was great to be able to give him a baptismal certificate to commemorate this solemn event. See the full story in the Addenda.

My roommate, James, has a wonderful godly mother. Even though he had accepted Christ some years earlier, he was discouraged and had neglected to read his Bible and pray. I suggested through Linda that it would be an encouragement to him to receive birthday cards, and people responded. He was overwhelmed that people who didn't know him at all would express love simply with a card. After receiving about a dozen cards he told me he was recalling feelings he had suppressed for years to be "other" oriented. God was truly warming his heart.

On Special Assignment

A few days later, he received a couple cards and a letter. He was so moved that people would write him out of simple genuine love because in his words, "these people have nothing to gain from me by them befriending me."

Super Bowl Sunday 2008 was an interesting day. Because the kitchen crew did not want to be left out, they prepared sack lunches for the evening meal and passed them out early. Several men also prepared special dishes in the dorm kitchen (basically a microwave). There was a rice dish, chicken wings, and shrimp. We enjoyed the eating, but learned not to ask question as to how that great food was able to get into our dorm!

Joseph shared in the service that afternoon how his sister had located his father's family. (He father had been in prison for about ten years, as had all his male siblings, and all his paternal cousins but one.) His sister helped facilitate a phone conversation with his grandmother who he had last seen at age six—well over twenty years before. His grandmother encouraged him to be the first to break the cycle of sin and stay out of jail once released.

Joseph was only eighteen when he came to prison. He had become a dynamic Christian before I met him. But we developed a great friendship and I became a counselor on many issues as he wanted to be prepared to live once he was on the "outside." We even talked about how to pick a mate, an occupation, and how to restore what Satan had deprived him of thus far in his life.

Another example of the injustice was found in Matt's case. He had a distinguished career in the military and served in administrative roles. He helped process various visas. He was charged with bribery and conspiracy. They alleged that a man bribed him to get a visa by giving him a motorcycle. But he had positive proof that he had purchased the motorcycle so they dropped that charge, but found him guilty on the conspiracy charge. That is mind-boggling because there was no conspiracy, and they could show no motive. Nevertheless, Matt survived this ordeal and was able to become a professor after his release. I continue to stay in contact with him.

As happened so often and without notice, our dorm was "shaken down." They ordered everyone out. Most of the men were made to strip their clothing, but all I got was a quick pat down. When they finished and we came back inside I noticed that nothing in our cubicle had been touched. Often the guards would simply throw everything on the floor and the inmate had to clean it up. Never mind that the written regulations required officers to put things back in the order they found them. Instead of complaining about being shut out, I simply went to the racquetball court and played for a couple hours.

I continued to fight high sugar. The numbers ranged from 150-200. That was in spite of my regular exercise—walking about 20+ miles a week and playing several hours of racquetball weekly. Part of the problem was that the BOP's record on providing medicine was abysmal. Often I would be without medicine for weeks at a time—and these medicines could be obtained from WalMart for $10 per three months. It was disgraceful.

I could write a whole book on the inconsistency of the kitchen. There were numerous reasons. One reason was that a lot of the good food was stolen between the warehouse and the camp kitchen. The theft was not only by inmates who could then sell it to other inmates, but by officers as well. On February 11, I noted that breakfast that morning was only oatmeal and leftover cherry cobbler.

My notes are riddled with an acronym, ACD. That stood for "Another Crazy Day." They called a fire drill, but they had to announce it on the loud speaker because the fire alarm went off so frequently that the men no longer paid any attention to it.

Whenever we could schedule it, we had a "pastors' meeting." We usually scheduled it for an hour in the evening. We averaged 6-8 in this meeting. The enthusiasm was usually high and often I would simply close the meeting after 1.5 hours.

There are several notations about being an ACD (another crazy day) repeatedly. They called an emergency count at 9:30p which substituted for the 10p count. I'm not sure what the 30 minutes gained them. They had just turned the lights out at 11p when they called another count. They had never cleared the previous count. ACD2. Then in the morning they called a "fog count" immediately after breakfast at 7a, but canceled it at 7:05a. ACD3. I came to the conclusion that so much of the government is an exercise in futility, and the BOP was at the bottom of that barrel.

The camp's religious diversity included Moslem, Hindu, Buddhist, Wiccan, and Jewish. There was a small Catholic contingency, as well as Orthodox. Then there were various strains of the mainline churches, Pentecostal, and all the varieties of Baptist. Avoiding heated discussions was intentional. God allowed me to establish relationships with all those groups, and I became known as "Pastor Bob." Sometimes various factions would employ me to be the mediator for all kinds of disputes. I couldn't always solve the issue, but I was able to calm spirits.

During all these months I was conversing with the attorney in Salt Lake City. I spent many hours in research, writing potential parts of the appeal case, and trying to get the attorney up to speed on tax issues. While there was promise of winning an appeal, I tried to keep a realistic understanding of the unjust courts in America, where the Appeals Courts are more concerned with protecting their own, than they are about administering justice.

There were other opportunities to minister to the sick. A man named Ernie had contracted cancer and the BOP medical procedures did little to help him. From mid-January to the first of March, he had lost thirty pounds. When he was finally so bad that he could hardly get around they shipped to a medical facility in Butner, NC.

Life was always in transition at the camp. Men were coming and going at the rate of ten per week. I gained a whole new understanding for the term "in limbo". Saying goodbye to men that had received spiritual help was difficult, especially not knowing whether I would ever have contact with them again. Then there was the challenge of constantly meeting new men and figuring out what needs they had and how God wanted me to help them.

Lee sensed that we needed more prayer time so he organized the men in the dorm who would meet in a circle format in the end of the dorm. This was done around 9p—between the 8p and 10p counts. We started small with six men. It quickly grew to up to 20 men. Each was encouraged to give their requests and then different men would bring those needs to the throne. It was exciting to see God answer many of those prayers, and the change in demeanor of the men whose prayers were answered.

One night Anthony was on the phone when the prayer group met. When he finished he came and asked Lee and me to pray for his sister, Deanna. He explained that in spite of their father being a pastor, they had gone into drugs together. He seemed to have broken the addiction, but she had not. So we had another prayer session.

A few days later, Anthony called his dad on Sunday night to tell him of his conversion. Naturally, his dad was thrilled. But his dad also told him that his sister, Deanna, had called him that same night we prayed for her. Her words, "I don't know what and you and Anthony are doing but I am a changed person." The desire for drugs and alcohol had left her in that same hour. Those kinds of answers to prayer excited others to more prayer! Anthony changed his telephone time so he could always be a part of the prayer circle.

Anthony then asked for prayer for God to help him with his cursing. He said the Spirit was checking him every time he started to curse. We began praying for complete deliverance. He accepted accountability for this cleansing.

March 20th found men gathering for special prayer. It was the day my attorney was to present the case before the Appeals Court. People all over the compound were praying that day. A special prayer session was called 15 minutes before that hearing. As we know, it was some time before we received the decision that we had been denied justice one more time.

We added some additional prayer time and we had Cedric lead. Cedric had been really foul-mouthed but had been publicly praying for help in this area. The prayer groups were times of great bonding and each night Cedric would hug me tightly and thank me for praying for him.

Good Friday was celebrated with a special service. I led the congregational music and Lee emceed. We had seven preachers on the last statement of Christ. Lee had assigned the topics out. Ironically, he had one wrong but no one other than me noticed. We had a good laugh about it later.

On Special Assignment

Time after time I became aware of personal struggles that men had when families or church families failed to give support to the inmates. One man, also named Bob, came to talk. His in-laws wavered in their support and sometimes, in his words, they were a "real pain." His brother, who was an Adventist minister had a hard time believing when Bob would tell him of the corruption in government—prosecutors, judges, etc. There was also the wickedness here in the staff. Fortunately, his wife and daughters, his parents and his local church were standing by him. I wish I could explain how important it is for that kind of support to be there. Even when someone has committed wrong, support is the best way to bring correction.

I could identify with these men to some degree. Compared to every man I knew there, my support system was overwhelmingly the best. It was only my one church connection where the bishop revealed his own wicked heart in joining those who condemn and destroy. But that was inconsequential in my case as day after day I received letters of encouragement.

Easter Sunday was a time for traditional worship. We sang, "Up from the Grave He Arose." Lee gave an altar call and two came forward to be saved, including Anthony with whom we had prayed on Friday night! Bob had been witnessing to Anthony as well as Lee. We further learned that Anthony's dad had once been a drug addict and that was the opening for his kids to get involved. His dad was saved later, and answered the call to preach.

On another night the prayer circle had twelve. There were more praises than requests. One report was a man getting 25 months taken off his sentence. Dr. Keith had requested prayer for a friend's little boy seriously injured in an accident, and he had made a miraculous recovery. Anthony reported attending the Bible study, and quoted his memory verses for us.

For many of these men, seeing an answer to prayer was a brand new experience. I often prayed that these times would make an indelible imprint on their hearts and create an unquenchable thirst for more of God.

Toward the end of March, we had requested that visitors for Sunday be allowed to attend the chapel service for Easter. We learned that morning that the assistant chaplain who was supposed to accompany the visitors had been fired because he was caught in a compromising situation with an inmate. It just shows the sick state of affairs (no pun intended) in government.

Another example of inconsistency was the newly assigned commanding officer for the quarter decided to shake down Dorm E to find cigarettes. Even though it is against the regulations for the officers to smoke on the premises, he was sucking a cigarette just before he entered the dorm. It is hypocrisy on steroids! ACD. I happened to be in the Visitor's Room when the shake down occurred and missed all that excitement!

Late in April, we scheduled a baptismal service with three candidates. We had just gone to service when an emergency count was called. It took 40 minutes. ACD2 since we had an emergency count that afternoon also. We returned to the chapel and the choir sang a couple songs. Then we did three baptisms—Anthony, Sidney, and Paul Richardson.

Another challenge was illustrated by Van. (He had tear drops tattooed on his cheeks.) He came to talk about his life. He has a wife and little daughter but I had never met them in the visiting room. He explained that their financial resources were very limited, and since he was getting out the next month, they had opted to not have visits these last few months so they would have adequate resources when he was released. He expressed many times how much he missed his wife and little girl.

Another man, who developed a friendship was Roy Bland, a mortician from South Georgia. He left on April 29 for 34 days in the half-way house. He thanked me for blessing his life while he was there. That same day Tom Duke and three others left. So the revolving door continued.

On May 6 I walked a mile with Ricky. He was serving a twelve-year sentence for drugs and was about half-way through it. He had disciplined himself to lose 80 pounds since January. He explained that his father had been a drunk who just got save about two weeks prior to his conversation. He quit drinking two weeks prior to that under conviction by the Holy Spirit. Ricky had never put his dad on his visitor's list. He also shared that he was able to sneak off the camp property and have a couple hour conjugal visit with his wife—first time since he had been in prison. He generally had been an obeyer of rules but over five years was a very long time. He considered the risk and felt it was well worth it.

One of the challenges that many inmates faced had to do with their "restitution." While almost all the judgments from the court required that they pay 10% of their net earnings on the restitution once they were out of confinement, the officer pushed for everyone to pay while they were still incarcerated. We guessed that they received some kind of bonus or recognition for doing so. Even if the rules were followed while in the camp, the $20 or so that they earned would only produce a payment of $2. But they put pressure on for each to ask friends and family to contribute so $25 or more could be paid each month. ACD plus! It was simply unjust, but typical of the BOP.

I noted on May 9 that I had been in Atlanta for 300 days. All through that time, I had prayed and hoped God would deliver, but it seemed in His providence that my "assignment" was not completed. It did not stop me from asking, "How long, O Lord, how long?"

In spite of the progress that many gained, the temptation to break the rules was always present. So Cedric was caught with his cell phone on afternoon when he had contacted his wife. They had him "packed out" and sent to the "hole" (cell confinement in the transfer center) within the hour. From there he would be shipped to a low security facility—the next step up from the camp (minimum security).

I was able to call my Mom on Mother's Day and she was so happy to talk with me. Others had already called and so I was able to get updated on my siblings in our 7-minute conversation.

Quite often there was friction with the various guards. One that we called "Parsons" was particularly annoying. At meal times, he insisted on sending everyone to their dorms and calling them in an order that he decided upon for that day. He seemed to think he could do it more orderly than the inmates but there had been no complaints. On this particular date, he decided that our dorm would be called last. He did not release us until 11:05a (I noted the time.) Standing in line and then getting through the food gathering,

I did not get to sit down to eat until 11:18a. At 11:30a Parsons starting yelling for everyone to be out. So I explained that he was unreasonable and that twelve minutes was not adequate to eat a main meal. He finally left which allowed me to take my cookies out of the dining hall or I would have been there a little longer. An hour later he stopped me to talk about it again but I held my ground, politely but firmly. ACD

There would be days when various religious groups would be served a special meal. Mother's Day and Pentecost happened to coincide. So at 2p that day, the Christians gathered in the dining hall for their special meal with fried fish and fried chicken. We even were able to take the extra food back to our dorm for later snacking.

Another interesting notation was the day an officer stole my little supply of bananas. I typically would buy a week supply for around $2. That officer came by my cube and saw them, and asked about them. I told him they were mine. Later when I was working on the other side of the room, he took them. When I went and asked for them back, he refused. That should show you how disgusting the character of some of the officers was that they would steal $2 worth of bananas from an inmate.

Often the kitchen was less than clean. One of the activities that we engaged in the evening was to go to the dining hall and watch the rats skate on the floor. When the place was officially inspected by outsiders, it was condemned. The inspectors required them to tear down the entire salad bar assembly and sanitize it. Several of the workers had to go in early to clean the rat droppings out of the kitchen before they could start fixing meals each day.

The rats were well fed. Even though rat traps were placed around the various buildings, the rats were so fat they could not get inside the traps, so they just pushed them around the yard trying to get at the bait.

The official inspection identified so many violations of cleanliness that the officers were jumping on the inmates to get things cleaned up. The Visiting Room (where I worked at the time) had the least infractions. There were some maintenance issues for which we were not responsible. There was a collection of dust behind some

On Special Assignment

of the vending machines so those had to be moved out and then cleaned behind them.

I often had men come to pour out their hearts because the "system" had been unfair. As repulsive as drugs are, the excessive sentences did little good for society or the men involved. One example, was John who received a 30-year sentence for simply flying another man to another state where he transacted a drug deal. Even though John was not involved in the deal at all, he was considered an accomplice. Another example was Sam, who received a 45-year sentence. A good attorney got it reduced to just 15 years. I was able to minister to him for the last year of his actual time of 13.5 years. I'll probably never see him again, but I trust I positively affected his life in some way.

We often had challenges getting people on the visiting list. Immediate family was supposed to be approved by simply listing them. Others had to fill out a form and have it vetted before getting approval to come. The officers were so inefficient (mostly lazy) that it took ten months for them to approve my sister and my mom to come. Once Allen and Rachel, my brother and sister in law, came who had not been previously approved. My other brother-in-law, Tim, told me of their coming so we went outside in the yard outside the visitor's center and visited through the fence. No guard came out to bother us so we spent about 20 minutes before they had to leave.

One of the motivations for people to continue to pray is to see answers to prayers. That was occurring regularly in our dorm prayer circle each night. A notation on May 28 was that Bob Mac who had asked for prayers for their financial needs reported. It was actually a two-fold prayer request. One, that God would provide to meet immediate needs, and second, that his wife would be willing to graciously accept them. His report was that both prayers had been answered. That same evening, Dr. Keith reported that prayer the previous night for his mother-in-law had been answered and that she was healed.

Another challenge was for an inmate name Michael C. He received word that his wife passed away the previous night—only 33 years of age. He was just three weeks from going home. The staff is so evil and lazy they would not process a furlough for him to go to his wife's funeral. Leaving time for the family to gather, the funeral was not scheduled for a couple weeks later which would only have left one week before his scheduled departure.

I received a request from my daughter, Sandi, to help with the youth camp devotionals since she and Tim were the directors. So that gave me some creative motivation and I prepared a full week of devotionals based on the theme she had selected.

The food was constantly a challenge. The hot water system in the kitchen broke, so they used paper supplies. Breakfast was a diabetic nightmare—very sweet frosted flakes—which after sitting in milk for 20 minutes were not the least soggy! One of the challenges for me was to not lose weight. The food was so bad that often I would not eat it. I went in the facility at 166 pounds, but after one year I was down to 159. It was not a significant weight loss, but nevertheless losing.

Part of the problem with the meals is that there was on-going theft of all the fresh fruits and vegetables. Kitchen and warehouse workers would steal the food and then sell it to the inmates who could afford to do so. So what they can't sell, or doesn't get stolen, that's the stuff that we got fed.

I made a note in June 2008 that my little toe was about to heal. The sore was the result of the BOP not supplying me with shoes that fit. Wearing a shoe that was seven sizes too wide wore blisters and then open sores during my first week there (July 2007). They were so severe that eleven months later, the last sore was just healing.

Every quarter there was a change of guards. One of the new evening guards, who was a professed Christian, said to the whole dorm one night, "I'll be on this quarter and my days off are Tuesday and Wednesday. So if you're going to go over the fence, please do it on those days." It was a little bit of levity, but he truthfully meant it.

It came time for Tim T to leave and go back to Florida. We had developed a relationship based on teaching in the PATH program. In the presence of both Robert Granda and Brent Tibbetts, who verified his statements, he said he had been told by five or six men that they believed the main reason they were allowed to come to prison was to meet me. None of those had talked to each other

On Special Assignment

when they told him. He went on to say that they, as well as he, believed I was the only role model they had met in prison they could follow. None of the other religious people had gained their full respect. He went on to say, "You have no idea how many lives you have impacted spiritually—and I'm one of them." It was a humbling moment for me, and I thanked him for his kind remarks. We never know who is watching. It was one of those times when God encouraged my heart even as I was struggling why God was not answering my prayers to be released sooner.

To fill the time, I did a lot of reading. Before I was confined, I averaged reading a book a week. With the extra time, I read even more. I noted that I was on schedule to read 120 books the first year in Atlanta at an average of 400 pages. That is nearly 50,000 pages and that did not count the Bible reading nor the legal research.

The last day of June, I noted that it was another SOS (same old silliness) at Camp Cupcake, as Raymond called it. Food was less than desirable. They served "chili mac" about 3 times a week. The hamburger they put in it has about a 40% fat content. The boxes the meat comes in are either labeled Grade F (which I had never heard previously) or "not fit for human consumption." Often it smells because of its age.

I was fortunate to get an exemption from the standard shoes—they are very reluctant to make any exceptions. So I wore tennis shoes the whole time I was there. The first pair was given to me and they were very used, but I was grateful. Not too long thereafter, Linda purchased me a proper pair and wore them into the visiting room. It was a little amusing since I wear a size 12 shoe so she stuffed the toes. Then we prudently exchanged shoes and she wore the used ones out.

I averaged walking three miles a day, sometime as much as five miles. Over a year's time, I walked close to 1000 miles. In addition, I played racquetball on the concrete court so after a year, the shoes needed replaced. So Linda wore another pair in and wore the worn-out ones out the door. It was the only way that it could be done.

The next challenge in the kitchen was that the oven was broken. The evening menu listed baked ziti, but without an oven that was out of the question. So they decided on chili-mac again except they had no macaroni. So they substituted flat noodles. The hamburger that night was 40% heart meat—not exactly delicious. The word on the "street" is that they had seriously mismanaged the budget so the substandard meals would be even worse until the end of the government's fiscal year (Sep 30). That would prove to be true.

The PA system was broken for some time. Some of the officers just loved to get on it and call people to do various things. Mostly it was annoying. So we all rejoiced when it was broken. The day came when it was working again, and Parsons and Ms. Terry were squawking the whole morning. Parsons even called a "fire drill." The actual fire alarm system was so bad that it went off several times daily. There were so many false alarms that no one paid any attention to it. But Parsons over the PA system required everyone to respond.

It was obvious from my notes that day after day I continued to express hope that I would be delivered soon. God, in His providence, did not come through, but continued to supply grace so that I could continue to minister to the various ones who came through there.

Walking was my consistent exercise. The track was a quarter mile and I walked it as many as 28 times in a day. Usually it was a minimum of 12 and often 20. With all that walking I eventually wore a hole in the toe of my tennis shoe. It was particularly annoying on rainy days—my big toe would get wet and the sock would turn Georgia mud red!

To fill in some of the time productively, occasionally we would gather in the music room and play gospel songs. There were several who played various instruments as well as guitars and we would have a very inspirational time. Tom Drummond from Alabama loved strumming his guitar, and "Moses" loved the singing. They finally got a new spinet piano placed in the music room, and that greatly increased people's desire to congregate there. So there were many who came to sing, as well as others who came to listen. David and I shared the time at the piano.

There were times when men would get transferred to other facilities. One was Ted who went to South Dakota. I knew another man there, Paul, and I made an introduction which proved beneficial for both men.

The prayer circle continued nightly, ranging from 3 to 12 men. Ike, a young man from Nigeria, testified. He grew up in Nigeria as a Catholic. When he moved to New York City, he was attracted to Brooklyn Tabernacle and attended until he moved to Atlanta. He strayed from the Lord and got in trouble with the law. In prison, he came back to the Lord and grew spiritually. That night he led in prayer.

August 2 will be a day etched in our memory forever. Linda was in town so I reported to the Visitor's Room for our Sunday visit. But she did not appear. I saw other friends come in and I was about to go out and make a phone call to her when Paula told me what had happened. Linda had fallen at a salon in Wal Mart the previous evening and shattered her left femur into eight major pieces. It created a whole new saga for several reasons. One, we did not have insurance at the time. Second, since she was in Georgia, none of the hospitals were willing to treat her. The emergency room did provide an inflatable cast so her leg could be immobilized.

It was our practice to have a short worship service on the lawn outside the visitor's center. That morning about 20 gathered. There were several prayer requests but Linda's accident was the primary focus. Jack led in Amazing Grace and I prayed the "pastoral prayer." Paula, Kenny's wife, was so kind as to provide me with lunch that day since Linda was not there. Jeremy, from Birmingham, who was visiting a friend offered to drive down from Birmingham to supply Linda with anything he could provide. That was an example of the comradery that develops between those involved in the in-justice system.

WHEN COMPLICATIONS BECAME A MAJOR FACTOR

Complications are always an opportunity for God to show himself strong. We were at a loss as to how to approach it. Shonna and RJ had come up with Linda that weekend. They had to go back home and did so, leaving Linda at her brother's home south of Atlanta. Our son-in-law, Chris, was a coach at Northside Christian School in St. Petersburg, FL. At practice, he was talking to his volunteer trainer about the incident. The trainer regularly worked for an orthopedic surgeon. He called his boss and told him the story. Dr. C obtained Linda's cell phone number and proceeded to call her. When the voice on the other end of the phone asked if this was Linda Bedford, she responded, "Who is this?"

The result of that conversation was that he told her, "Get yourself back to St Petersburg, and I will see that you are taken care of and you won't have to worry about the money." Truly, Dr. C that day was the "voice of God." She lived with this air cast for a week. The next weekend the girls came and picked up Linda and she returned to St Petersburg where Dr. C had arranged for a week's stay in Bay Front Hospital. He furthered arranged for all the other specialists needed for the surgery. The repair job required a platinum plate to which all the major pieces of bone were attached. It then required to harvest some bone to graph in places where pieces were too small to put back together. There was complete follow up as well. It was extremely challenging to me, knowing that I could not offer any assistance.

This began a five-month process where Linda started out in a wheel chair, graduated to a walker, then to a cane. The process was not fun, and our girls were there to help when she could not do for herself. The therapy was long and grueling. I am delighted to report that Dr. C was a miraculous surgeon and that Linda has no residual negative effects from the injury.

The night after she had the surgery, I was able to talk with her by phone but she sounded awfully groggy. Even then she was very positive about the surgery, and looked forward to the healing. She had no way of calling in to me, and I carefully used my ten minutes a day allotment to the best use.

On Special Assignment

The men were very expressive toward Linda and sent "hand-made" cards that were artfully crafted. Dozens of men signed those cards and that was indicative of the love and prayers that were sent her way.

Meanwhile, I was expressing hope that the Appeals Court would soon rule in my favor. At that time, it had been twenty weeks since the oral arguments were presented. The wait times are completely ridiculous and appear to provide harm to those seeking justice.

The Tuesday after Linda's incident I finally was scheduled for an EKG. It was a good thing I told the nurse my cardiac history because the EKG is always "abnormal." My heart attack in 1999 had altered the graph, but it remained consistently "abnormal" ever since. The amazing part is that the EKG is a part of the "entrance exams" and this was occurring some 13 months after admittance. More ACD!

My notes express the frustration I felt for not being home to assist Linda in her rehabilitation. My daughters all assured me they would tend to her every need and they were there faithfully. The healing that occurred is a testimony to Linda's determination and our daughters help.

On August 6, I noted that the evening OIC was either drunk or crazy. He made a huge fuss the previous night about smelling cigarette smoke when he did the evening count. He sent everyone down to one end and then proceeded to search some of the cubes but found none. The next day he was in the dining hall yelling obscenities that no one was to say a word—only eat. He was carrying a baseball bat threatening to beat inmates if they crossed him. ACD!

To finish that evening, for the 8pm the OIC ordered us all outside, then we had to re-enter the dorm one by one. Apparently, he couldn't stay on count because he used a clicker to keep track. More example of ACD!

One evening I had a conversation with a Hispanic guy from Houston. He wanted more information about baptism. Then he shared his "story." His cousins from New York stopped by en route to Mexico and counted money they had made from a drug deal. Narcs had followed them to his house and he was arrested on a conspiracy to launder money even though he had nothing to do with any of the cousins' business. But he was scared by the prosecutors, and agreed to a plea deal in which he got eight years. The end result was the destruction of his marriage.

The constant flow of men in and out of the camp was interesting. An average of ten weekly was the count. There were men from all walks of life. Even though about 70% were African Americans, there were some from several different countries in Africa and Asia. The dorm where I was housed had a normal capacity of 72. They had as many as 76 stuffed in there, but by August of 2008 we were down to 60.

There was a man from South Korea named Shen. He was the kindest, meekest gentleman on the compound and a godly man. His "crime" was helping other Koreans get to the US. At first, they charged him with terrorism. That was so ludicrous they dropped that and just left him with VISA fraud. Compared to the immigration nonsense of today, he would certainly be viewed differently.

Day after day it seemed my life was one counseling session after another. There was marriage counseling. In a report by FSU Criminology they stated, **"The longer the inmate is in prison, the more likely the marriage is to fail.** One recent study found that each year of incarceration increases the odds that the inmate's marriage will end in divorce (before or after the inmate gets out of prison) by an average of 32 percent." That was certainly true of the men I was with on a daily basis. Since I had little to no contact with the spouses, the emphasis was all on improving their relationship to God.

There were all other kinds of counseling as well: financial including tax issues; bereavement; personal discipline, especially thought life; bitterness; self-pity; and especially religion. I had the privilege of working with those of the Jewish faith, Moslem, Hindu, Buddhist, Wiccan, as well as all the varieties of Christianity. God's Word was my foundation, and its truth proved itself for all to see. There were days when I spent up to six hours in counseling.

It seemed that at least 50 men per day would ask about my wife and the healing of her leg. They would all assure me they were praying for her regularly.

On Special Assignment

In the middle of August, I received word the Appeals Court had denied my appeal. For a couple days I fought the disappointment. But on the 15th I recorded that God sent a peace into my heart. I didn't know at that point whether that was a hope of a new miracle, or if God had a longer plan for serving there. The latter would prove to be true and God would supply the grace.

I mentioned earlier about the officer who was threatening the men with a baseball bat. When some of the top officials walked through the compound, they were stopped and informed of this officer's bad behavior. So he was upset and came to the various units spewing out retaliatory words. When he got to the dorm where Judge Wes resided, he jumped upon the short wall and lambasted those there, demanding to know who "turned him in." Judge stepped forward and said, "I did." He ordered him to go to the OIC office where they had a 30-minute conversation. The full story would be too long, but the officer wilted when Wes told him he prayed for him nightly. He responded and told Wes he respected him for stepping forward. His behavior did modify over the next few weeks.

Celebrating our 40th anniversary was by mail and telephone since Linda was unable to travel during this time. She responded well to the surgery and actually healed well ahead of schedule, but it just seemed like a long time. Tim and Susan did extra visiting during that time, and it was greatly appreciated.

My daily reading of the Bible brought me to this verse, and it spoke volumes to me that day. Zephaniah 3:20, "I will give you renown and praise among all the peoples of the earth when I restore your fortunes before your eyes, says the Lord." It seemed a promise just for me—the unanswered question was "when?"

On an irregular schedule, men from the Internal Security department would come to the camp. They would come running in and order everyone against a wall. They would pat each one down and then send us outside for two hours. It was usually a ritual before holidays as they tried to stop any drug/alcohol parties. My locker was not disturbed but the report was they confiscated 37 cell phones, 80 cartons of cigarettes, 150 2 oz. bottles of liquor, 20 large bottles of liquor, 2 DVD players, and one laptop with internet connections. They were unable to identify the owner of the contraband so no one went into confinement.

Bob Bedford

My big toe had worn a hole in my tennis shoe—it only had about 1000 miles of walking, plus 200 hours of racquetball on concrete surface. So I needed a new pair but Linda was still unable to travel. So Susan became the courier. She wore the new pair of tennis shoes in—even though it looked a little odd, no one questioned her. When the guards were busy looking elsewhere, we made the switch and she wore the old ones out and then threw them away. It's a shame such tactics had to be employed just to survive!

The food was so bad at times in the dining hall that I was glad to stay in the dorm and have ramen noodles. Several times the lunch meat would be turning green. One day it was what seemed like pieces of Styrofoam for breakfast cereal, then fried chicken livers, that smelled half rotten, and watery instant potatoes for lunch. Supper was their take on chili-mac with the heart-meat hamburger. It was more than I could stomach.

I was constantly introduced to cases where the government had manufactured a crime. Men would bring me their entire trial transcripts to read. Another one of those was Charles Edwards. The case against him was ludicrous. He had a payphone business with several investors. The payphone business collapsed when the cell phones gained traction. A cell phone booth is now a relic of the past, if you can even find one. The government accused him of a crime for the failed business, calling it conspiracy. The government was unable to name a second person involved so the indictment read with "persons unknown." It amazes me every time a jury convicts someone like this. He was already a senior citizen before he was accused and the judge gave him a ten-year sentence. As a testimony of God's grace, Charles maintained a great attitude and continued to shine for Jesus.

Again, and again we were searched for contraband. On a day in September they called an emergency count at 7:20am. Extra officers were brought in to help search. Things remained locked down until 11a and only then were we permitted to go to lunch. They patted us down as we left the dorm. After lunch, we were sent to the recreation yard while they finished their search. I took a book with me so I walked two miles and read. It was 12:20p before we were okayed to go back to the dorms. They had messed up a lot of the cubes (which, in itself, was a violation of regulations). My bed was messed up where they had lifted the mattress to search. We were not given the "all clear" signal until 1:15p. This day deserved a double ACD!

One of the men I really appreciated was Vinnie. He was a chiropractor and would give free adjustments. There were many health professionals there and each one was helpful in some way or another. Dr. Ben examined my swollen ankles and diagnosed it as tendonitis. He recommended that I do more stretching before racquetball or intense exercise. So I tried to heed that advice.

Sept 6 was a milestone because Linda was finally able to come for a visit. All the men who were in the visitor's room greeted her warmly. It had been five weeks since her accident, and she came in a wheel chair. Just to see her brought cheers from us all. Almost everyone in the room had been praying for her (even those of other faiths).

Todd sent me a book by Brother Yun, "The Heavenly Man." He was a Chinese national involved in the house church movement that has been so successful. It was very encouraging reading. From prison he wrote, "God has sent me to be His witness in this place. There are many people who need Jesus. I will be in this prison for exactly the length of time God has determined. I won't leave one moment early and I won't stay one moment too long. When God determines my ministry in prison is complete, I will come out." You can visit his website at www.backtojerusalem.com.

As my birthday rolled around again, my mailbox was full of birthday cards. So many men are forgotten while incarcerated! Over the first few days of September I received about 75 cards. Each one of those represented a family or friend who was praying for me and the ministry that God had allowed while there.

In mid-September I received word that the Appeal Court had turned down my appeal. It was obvious that they did not consider the facts and were simply upholding the lower court's denial of justice. Most of the points made in the appeal were not even addressed, and they simply cast aside my motion in broad sweeping statements. That caused us to rethink the future. While I did have the opportunity to submit a 2555 appeal, it would first go before the same judge who had been so unfair in the first place. It is almost impossible to even get a fair hearing much less justice. A final nail in the coffin of this process was that the judges simply failed to act and so by doing nothing, an additional avenue for justice was denied.

The Moslems celebrate Ramadan each year, and the BOP accommodates them to the max. They fast during the daylight hours and then they are fed an enormous meal after dark. There were only about 25 Moslems in the camp, but they fixed a special meal each night for 30 days. They usually had more than they could eat so they would bring excess to the dorm. Because I had gained favor with several of the Moslems, they would share their excess with me.

Often I would be stopped at various places around the camp for people to share a prayer request or ask for counsel. One day Joshua stopped me and told me how much the message the previous week had meant to him. In fact, he could give me the basic outline of every message he had heard me preach. He concluded by saying, "You're different because you live what you preach and that makes it powerful." It was only by God's grace that I could live it.

My role was sometimes in church discipline. Pastor Greg received a report about Chico, and he came immediately to me. As is instructed in Matthew 18, we went to Chico and told him the accusations. He denied them, but did not seem defensive. Convinced that the accusations were not true, we began to trace the source. Someone had made an assumption based on Chico trying to befriend the unsaved. So Greg and I met with those who had perpetrated the accusation and they agreed it was a misunderstanding. They went and apologized and the relationships were resolved. Even in a prison camp, following Christ's instructions always produce good results.

On a visitation day in October, a decision was made to lock down the visiting room and strip search all the inmates. That day Susan had brought me some Efferdent for my false teeth. I had not anticipated the lock down so, of course, the guard found the "contraband.' He grabbed it and threw it on the floor. When I went back to clean the after the count, the Efferdent was still there on the floor, so I picked it up and took it safely back to my locker.

On Special Assignment

I became pretty adept at cooking apples. We used the microwave in the dorm, and I learned the proper timing. Having access to butter and cinnamon made them tasty. Apples were usually plentiful so the men would bring me extra apples in exchange for some "baked apples." It seemed to be a special treat in the midst of so much distasteful food.

Mail call was a special time for me because I always received mail—a rarity for most of the men. I had been there 15 months before there was a two-day gap in receiving mail. Getting that much mail was a testimony to the others of the great support base that I had, but it also witnessed to them of my innocence and many expressed those sentiments.

Maintenance was a joke most of the time. The ice machine broke down and it took weeks to get it fixed. At the same time, the drain in the laundry room was clogged so they stopped anyone from doing laundry there. The cause of the clog turned out to be the excessive cigarette butts that were thrown there to be hidden from the guards. In addition, the cable TV was broken for several days and that always caused a lot of unrest since many of the men were addicted to TV. In addition, almost all the buildings leaked so rainy season was particularly annoying. If the residents weren't doing some maintenance, it would have been miserable indeed.

On October 28, I received the news that I had become a great-grandfather. Our granddaughter, Kasi, had a little girl whom she named Ava June. It didn't make me feel any older. I was glad everyone was fine after the event and I would look forward to the day when I would see her and hold her in person. When I shared the news, everyone rejoiced. They seemed to adopt her as part of their family and I was glad to consider them all a part of my family.

The man who had been the assistant law library clerk left for the half-way house on October 29, and that left that position open. Since my roommate was the head clerk, he recommended me to get that position, and the counselor had no objection. There were many benefits to switching job assignments and so that became a reality. I would now have a permanent desk there and be able to do personal research as well as help the many men who would need assistance.

My first 483 days there I was assigned to the Visitors' Room clean up detail. I was glad to move on from that craziness. They cut those assigned there by almost half so the work load was increasing. The supply line was erratic—we could not get regular deliveries of cleaner, wax or even a spray bottle for weeks. Going to work was a challenge because they had to open the gate, and most of the time the guards were too lazy to do it timely. Sometimes they called the 4p count at 3:05p on visitation days so the work had to be done later—sometimes after supper.

The fall schedule for the PATH program had me teaching a course on how to become to build a home inspection program. Part of the materials had been prepared by attorney Charles who left me all his materials. Having built a house from the ground up, most of the information I was teaching I had also experienced firsthand. At least, it gives the men an option for a career once they leave here.

Several men had asked about me teaching them the piano, but most of the time they did not follow through. Then Henry came and persisted so I begin teaching him some of the rudiments of theory and had him begin by practicing the scale in the key of C with his right hand. Sure enough I found him in the music room practicing every day for at least 30 minutes. The next week, at his lesson, he progressed right on beginning the C scale with his left hand. We changed the schedule to having 5-10 minute lessons three times a week. Because of his consistent practice and his unquenchable desire to learn, he was able to become a reasonably good pianist in less than four months.

When there was a lot of contraband found, or other violations of expectations, the manager would cancel visitation. Since morale was at a very low level anyway, having visits canceled exasperated the situation. It was especially crazy because when a few had violations they punished everyone. Often they were unable to determine who the violators were because of their own incompetence. To punish everyone further lowered morale, so the days following a cancellation there were even more violators. They reasoned that if everyone would get punished whether guilty or not, they might as well be guilty.

The craziness never stopped; it just took different forms. In late November, the officer on duty wrote down a wrong census number

On Special Assignment

for our dorm—we had 54, but he wrote down 57. So at the 3am count, he thought we were three short. So he turned on all the lights, ordered everyone standing with their ID cards. They began another count. Halfway through, we heard the lieutenant speak through his radio that the correct number was only 54. So he quickly said, "Sorry, guys" and hi-tailed it out of there. ACD!

The third weekend in November, Kasi was able to bring Ava to meet her great-grandfather. She was a very good baby for the day, and, of course, she attracted incredible attention from all the men. Not quite a month old, she became "real" to me—not just a picture.

One of the mental processes that many go through is "survival." There was nothing in the BOP that was uplifting, much less redemptive. For me, it was to keep busy. Reading, writing, counseling, exercising, playing the piano or singing, or researching. I watched no TV nor did I waste time playing mindless games. While I needed some rest from the heavy work schedule I had maintained for many years, the level of frustration dealing with the incompetence and indifference of those in charge was monumental.

Moving to the Law Library for my work was wonderful. I had a nice desk and chair which greatly facilitated my work. Since it was centrally located on the grounds, it was a meeting place. Although not large, it would accommodate about 20 men at a time. It also allowed me to connect in many ways since many of them had legal or tax issues to resolve. Life troubles are almost always connected to spiritual issues so I could segue right into conversations about God's truth.

Thanksgiving Day we had a wonderful meal. It included sliced turkey, sliced ham, cornbread dressing/gravy, candied yams, yeast rolls, and pumpkin pie. We knew we had to enjoy them because it would not be repeated anytime soon. To let the kitchen workers off the rest of the day, they passed out sack lunches for our supper than day.

December began with more of the routines: research and legal work, tax work, counseling, teaching, writing and exercise. Linda had been in her "healing" mode since the accident back in August. It had been a major ordeal, starting out with a wheel chair. She was unable to go to the bathroom by herself, and the girls were so good to be helpful. When she came to visit back in September she needed to stay in a hotel where they had "handicapped access." Staying at her brother's home was not practical due to the steps. During that time, she was not allowed to put any weight on the leg where she received the bone grafts.

She was finally able to graduate to a walker after three months. Then to crutches, next to a cane. She progressed steadily and by December she was able to visit without these assistance aids. She had previously sent me a copy of her X-rays. The doctor friends there commented on the superior job that her surgeon had done.

During these weeks, I was also scheduled to attend the "pre-release program." They covered a variety of topics but most of the information was completely irrelevant, not only to me, but to most. But that is typical of our government's approach, particularly the BOP. They interpret activity as progress.

It was always interesting that I was able to use all my available time productively. When I wasn't on a particular assignment from God, I was able to read. I've always been an avid reader and regularly read 50 books a year. But here I was able to up that to about 10 books a month. This included a lot of novels for the first time in my life. I had for several years made myself read at least one novel a year. Since novels were readily available and other books of my interest were not, I read more novels than all previous years of my life.

One of the things that amazed my friends here in Atlanta was the faithfulness of my friends to stay in touch and be supportive. Christmas time was especially fruitful in receiving mail. Letters and cards were more abundant than ever. I freely shared my correspondence with others so they, too, could be blessed. Many received no mail at all—especially those who had been incarcerated a long time. I was often reminded of the scripture, Hebrews 13:3, "Remember the prisoners, as though in prison with them, and those who are ill-treated, since you yourselves also are in the body." One interesting insight to me was that it did not matter whether someone is in prison justly or unjustly, we are still to treat them the same.

On Special Assignment

Doc received a letter from Rodney who had been transferred to the drug program in the Talladega facility. He had already joined a bible study group and even more importantly, had begun reconciliation with his wife. That was a "miracle" given the hopelessness that it seemed a short time before. It was an encouragement to all the believers here.

It was December and it was cold. When I was called to come to visitation, I was informed that we were not to wear a coat. It was too much of bother for the guard to check us out. I considered it inhumane to bear the cold air to go to the visitor's room. As rundown as my immune system was from the poor diet, poor sleep, and excess stress, it was not surprising that I constantly fought off a cold during the winter months.

On December 16, I made a notation that it was 520th day of incarceration. What we thought was the worst-case scenario was another 380 to go. It would prove to be a little longer than that based on situations that occurred late during the time.

Linda felt moved to send a card to the mother of Tyler, over in Alabama. She was so moved, she read the whole thing to her son twice, and he was reduced to tears. I wish others could learn that it takes so little to make a major impact on people's lives. Never miss an opportunity to do good and be kind!

It seemed unprovoked at times, but that did not stop the officers from calling a lock down census (which we labeled "senseless"). Often it would take them hours to make the count. One of the small blessings was that if a disagreeable officer was assigned to us, in three months they would rotate off. Knowing that often relieved some of the stress—just survive a few more weeks.

Eighteen months was not long enough for maintenance to fix the fire alarm system. I noted on the 19th that the alarm had gone off ten times, and every one of them a "false alarm." One of life's maxims is that "too many false alarms causes people to ignore all of them."

I received letters from the "outside" asking spiritual questions as well. I took every one of them seriously, and gave careful biblical answers. Written answers often are weightier than verbal because they can be re-read multiple times and pondered.

You've heard the expression, "it takes all kinds." One fellow who was simply called "Pudding"—I never did learn his real name—came into the chapel where I was practicing on the piano. He knew about my severe cold that had plagued me for some time. He told me God had sent him to anoint me. So he brought out a jar of olive oil and poured some on my head. Then he placed both hands on my head and prayed for about five minutes for my healing. He was very sincere, and I thanked him for it.

Christmas Day, 2008, came and my brother-in-law Tim, along with my friend, Geoff Marott came around 9am for a nice visit. Other friends smuggled me some Nyquil capsules to assist my healing process. When they left, we went for the dinner which was a little Cornish hen as the main entrée. Dessert was a slice of apple pie with a little drizzle of caramel chocolate.

We had a chapel service at 1pm. Mike helped me with the announcements and readings. We had requested that families be allowed to come down, but that was nixed by the administration. So we only had seven in attendance, but we had a nice time of communion and I gave a Christmas devotional.

Saturday was a visitation day, and Linda and Teri came with Rudy, my grandson who was then seven months old. Everyone in the visiting room agreed as to how "cute" Rudy was. It is impossible to explain how edifying visits are, and how demoralizing it is when someone has no one to care enough to come visit.

The month was fast closing and I was still dragging physically. I noted on the 29th that I was able to ride the bike for 15 minutes—the first time since December 12. The night before I opened the chapel service, but did nothing else. The outside group decided to let Chico preach since that was his final night at this camp. The next morning, he was transferred to the camp at Talladega AL.

The year end came. It was another day of meeting new men and each one seemed to have a spiritual need, and so sought counsel. I didn't always have an answer, but I could always pray and ask God for wisdom and help. Health was still slowly improving, but it was a

On Special Assignment

struggle. There was an opportunity to play racquetball but because of the cold weather, and my poor stamina, I only lasted ten minutes.

It was commissary day. They were scheduled to open at 12:30p, but typical of the BOP employees, it was 2:35pm before they opened. Then many of the officers felt it was their duty to harass the men. "Parsons" stopped me in the lunch room and asked, "What's wrong with your feet?" It was his indirect way of asking for my "soft shoe permit." The normal attire was the black brogans that were issued to each. But since the narrowest size they had was EE, it was a major problem. I wear a 12AA. So the only way to cope was to get a permit to wear tennis shoes all the time.

It was also a sad day because Tyler received word that his father had passed away. It is always tough to lose your father, but doubly so when you are incarcerated. I spent some time with him that afternoon talking perspective. I had lost my father 20 years prior to that so I had some understanding. His counselor agreed to request a furlough for him to attend the funeral.

That day six new men were taken in. One was assigned to our dorm, so I could help with orientation. Tom shared that he had a 41-month sentence, so I understood some of the things he would be facing. With nothing else happening, I did not stay up to welcome the New Year!

2009 January

New Year's Day was nothing spectacular. I was still fighting the cold. I was unable to get any medical help from the doctor on duty. They did give me some "medicine" but it was totally ineffective. So I continued to cough profusely at times, and that was very tiring. Since it was a Thursday, we had a regular chapel service, and Pastor Clarke did the speaking.

I was still battling what I later found out was pneumonia. Normally, the medical department would take a chest x-ray to do a correct diagnosis. The machine was inoperative at the time so that was delayed. It affected my energy significantly and I resorted to frequent naps.

There was a significant amount of fog during January so the BOP resorted to "fog counts" frequently, up to three times a day. The purpose was to ascertain that none of the men has walked away in the fog. The counts caused all kinds of disruption including locking the gate to the visitors' room. On that particular Saturday, the lieutenant in charge must have been bored with nothing productive to do.

At other times the guards would put up a bluff. When we were leaving the visitors' room, the officer lock the gate back to the dorms. He informed us that a strip search crew was on its way and it would be done in the admin building. He said, "if you have any contraband, I advise you to throw it on the ground before they get here." No one seemed to care, and after five minutes he unlocked the gate and everyone left without even being patted down.

On the next day as we were leaving the visitors' room, they stopped everyone to do a pat down. They took my ball point pen and even grabbed my well-used handkerchief. He found my book of stamps, but one was already missing so he didn't label it as "contraband" but he took it anyway, making sure everyone heard it. But when I went outside, he followed me and gave them back. Later when I went up to get my other things, one of the orderlies had retrieved my pen and gave it back.

I continued to struggle medically and it brought night after night of fitful sleep. I coughed throughout day and night. Others brought me various kinds of medicine but none of it was effective. Ward, a medical doctor, suggested that I go to the Medical Call office and demand an x-ray, but he was quite sure that I had pneumonia. Dr. Mike confirmed the diagnosis, but the office would not get any medicine to properly treat it, so I suffered on. Meanwhile, my sugar counts jumped to over 200.

I would often take naps of an hour or more several times a day. Anyone who knows me knew this was totally out of character. But I just didn't have the energy to do otherwise. Several guys gave me extra oranges so I could load up on natural vitamin C. A visit to the physician's assistant, confirmed my problems. I had a fever, my blood pressure was elevated (155/91), my pulse was 97, and my sugar was over 200. The x-ray machine was still not fixed so he couldn't confirm the pneumonia after listening to my breathing. He prescribed two medicines, one an anti-biotic and another one for the coughing. After a week on this antibiotic, my lungs were still

On Special Assignment

scratchy. It was so difficult to maintain eating when I did not feel good, and so my weight dropped to 142 fully clothed—a loss of 24 pounds from my check-in weight.

Ineffective results from the prescribed medicine led to desperation. One night I had talked to Linda via a borrowed cell phone about the situation. One risked a lot by talking on the authorized phone system because all calls were monitored. I explained how I was getting much worse. My roommate, James, called Linda immediately afterwards (unknown to me at the time) and emphasized how much I needed help.

Linda mobilized her "forces" and, in contact with medical doctors in the area, was able to get a prescription that would prove to be what I needed. The next challenge was "how to get it delivered" to me. But where there's a will, there is a way. It took the cooperation of more than one person, but the medicine was delivered safely to me. Even though the normal cost of one pill was $150, God provided it at no cost. Within three days, the pneumonia was healed, and within five days the cough was gone.

I continued to send requests for bibles to our benefactor in Colorado. One young man, Warren, came and thanked me for his new bible. He was a quiet shy black who had wanted a study bible but was afraid to ask. He finally worked up enough courage to come ask. His smile that day revealed his grateful heart.

That month, one of the most obnoxious guards was escorted off the camp because he had tried to plant evidence of drugs on a new inmate. Whether it was confirmed or not, he returned in a few days. Another inmate was sent to the Special Holding Unit (SHU) because he had brought candy from the visitors' room to his cubicle. But he was returned to the camp in a few days. There was this constant nonsense in the administration of the camp—sometimes hour to hour.

It was Tyler's turn to leave for a half-way house. His mother decided to do it with class so she rented a limo to drive him to Birmingham. Because of other screw-ups the staff had done, they tried to compensate by giving him seven hours to report, which allowed extra stops if they wished such as having a great restaurant meal.

Getting back to exercise was very difficult—fighting fatigue and low energy. I was able to get back on the track walking for a couple laps (half-mile) late in January after a three-month layoff. I also tried playing a little racquetball but that was very much a challenge.

The kitchen was always a challenge to me trying to find enough edible items to stay somewhat healthy. The place had been invaded by bugs for some time, and the administration finally decided to do something about it. They sprayed the entire place significantly on Friday night. By Monday morning, the men were picking bugs or bug parts out of their oatmeal. A true health inspector would have shut this place down in a minute.

The men were alert to news about legislation or regulations that would be favorable to them. But the promises from the politicians were short-lived. They were big on talk and short on delivery. Even the election of Obama was viewed by the groups there to be positive. As far as I can determine, almost nothing was ever accomplished in this regard.

Late in January, I noticed that I was on the "call out sheet" (which reported scheduled medical appointments). It gave a time for me to receive an x-ray. After having been there 18 months, I still had not received my x-ray which was a part of the entrance exams. But that week I did get the x-ray, and since I had received the medicine and been healed the week before, nothing unusual showed up on the x-ray. In my notes, I labeled it "hypocrisy."

To show you some of the idiocy that we were forced to live with daily. When the quarter passed, the new officer for the kitchen was Allen. I wrote in the journal that "the only description that comes to mind is the "village idiot." He was late every morning for breakfast. Once he got there it took him 45 minutes to open a box of cereal, get donuts out of the freezer, and set out the apples and milk. He bellowed like a dying cow. This particular morning, he finally opened at 6:20am (only 20 minutes late.) The men came out of the cold, and then he lectured them all saying he had no respect for the campers. So he sent them all back out, and as soon as everyone was out, he called them all back in.

Quite often the items which were listed on the menu were not available because guys in the warehouse would steal them in order to sell them to men on the camp. John reported to me one day that 80 loaves of bread were missing.

On MLK day, 2009, they served a dessert for lunch which was an apple pie. However, it also contained walnuts. Torrance, a nice young professional from the area, ate a piece not knowing it also had walnuts. He was highly allergic to nuts and collapsed in front of C dorm. His breathing stopped. Joshua, who had been a medic in the army (including two terms in Iraq) gave his mouth-to-mouth resuscitation while officers summoned an ambulance. He reacted so strongly that his bowels let loose and made quite a mess. He was transported to the hospital and stayed for three days. Ironically, a breathing device hung on the wall about fifteen feet from where he collapsed. However, the BOP has a rule that in order to use it, four trained officers must be present. Since there are almost no times that four officers are present, it hangs there as wall decoration.

February 2 was an eventful day. I had been able to return to racquetball after a three-month layoff. Thirty minutes into play that day I tripped as I was going after a low and wide shot. The court there was an open court of concrete with only the one wall to hit off. I knew immediately that I was injured so I reported immediately to medical. They took three x-rays but could find no broken bones. However, I had a protrusion of about ¾ inch sticking up from my right shoulder which they could not explain. The PA gave me some pain medication and told me to return the next morning.

I then went to Doc Mike for help in diagnosing it. It was very strange and he suggested that it was either a dislocation or a detached (torn) tendon. He believed an MRI would be essential for a complete diagnosis. Getting an MRI which would require a trip to an outside facility which was almost impossible to get. Many gathered to pray for me, and I had numerous offers of additional pain medication. This began a saga which would not be complete for almost a year.

With the help of the pain medications, I was able to sleep. The next morning I returned to medical for the radiologist to read the x-rays. Of course, damage to soft-tissue does not show up on x-rays. The plan of action was to wait a few days. The protrusion had decreased and I could move my arm more freely except for raising it high. Stay tuned for the further developments.

Jabari wrote a novel and had it published while he was there. He asked me to review his manuscript and I was able to catch a lot of items, including some spelling. The story was set in the black drug culture of Atlanta, with all its jive. I read the book and wondered how much of the book was based on reality. He confirmed that most of it was a true story. He was very good with descriptive adjectives and planned to keep writing on the "outside."

Chapel services continued to be a point of inspiration. When there was not an outside speaker, Greg and I shared the pastoral leadership. Even though we were provided with the names of those who should have come, about 50% of the time no one showed. The black choir and our Southern Gospel quartet continued to provide the special music. It was very exciting when I was able to pass out the baptismal certificates for those we had baptized the prior weeks.

My shoulder continued to give me problems. I could feel and hear bones moving against each other with certain movement. I had no idea what was wrong, I just knew it was. It often was so painful I could not sleep. When I went to medical, the PA showed me the radiologist's report, but all it said was "slight shoulder separation." He could offer me nothing other than pain pills. He did promise to talk with the doctor and try to get me a referral to an orthopedist.

Counseling was in constant demand. Often it was marriage counseling. David had gone through several phases of feeling loved and then rejected by his wife. He came by my cube seeking guidance on how to respond to his wife the next day in visitation. My counsel that day was for him to trust God to change her heart and then to respond as if he had. He reported back after the visit that she was radically different. She wore a Pink Valentine T-shirt and pictures taken with David and the whole family. She said she had enrolled the kids in church activities-basically the very things he had prayed would come to pass. He was flabbergasted, and had to spend considerable processing these new beginnings. It certainly bolstered his faith.

One evening "Coffee John" came to my cube exploding with rage. Tensions had been building for some time between him and Earl, both long-termers. John had been incarcerated for 16.5 years, and Earl for 17.5 years. There was no real issue other than personal

On Special Assignment

insults. If they engaged in an actual fight, they would lose a lot of their "good time" and be shipped to a higher security facility. After hearing John rant, I took another twenty minutes to calm him down. Hearing his own rage verbally helped him to see how foolish it was.

Every so often, the facility would be subject to "inspection." At no other time, did any of the staff desire to keep up with maintenance items. The kitchen and dining hall was routinely neglected so at this time they had major cleaning to do. They moved the tables outside (remember it was February and very cold). They would serve the meals on Styrofoam. They stripped the floors but not until Friday on a holiday weekend (Valentine's Day). The man with the machine could not finish the job timely so it remained unfinished through Monday evening. Only in Atlanta could we have such erratic administration.

The notes for the month of March indicate the challenge of living above the drudgery. There was the challenge of getting a good night's sleep. Often the guards would come in to do their midnight count and turn the lights on because they forgot their flashlight. Another night they came in and informed a man he was being transferred to another facility (his request of ten months previous) and that he had two hours to pack and be ready to go. That caused many to get up and give him a "goodbye."

One of my huge challenges was to find enough decent and nutritious food to keep my sugar in check as well as not lose weight. It took discernment for every meal. Fortunately, the other men were accommodating. I would regularly trade food items that I couldn't eat for things that others did not like.

There was also the challenge of overseeing the bible study groups development as well as the chapel services. I became the "go to guy" for various disputes, especially between the various religions—a small but vocal Moslem group, Buddhists, Hindus, Wiccans, and Jews. The various divisions of Christianity were just as challenging: Catholics, Baptists, Methodists, Charismatics, Seventh Day Adventists, and many others. Somehow God helped maintain civility through it all.

The source of beginning so many Bible study groups was the Bible program. The Stimacks in Colorado supplied study Bibles for anyone willing to engage in daily discipleship, and actively start a Bible study group in their dorm. Over the course of the 34 months, over 75 Bible study groups were started. But many had no previous training in scripture and none in spiritual leadership. So we had leadership training groups meeting weekly. I facilitated some of them as did the other ministers and laymen.

Almost all the medical service was a joke. It was hard to even get an appointment and when it did happen, most of the time there was no real help. Getting simple medicine like metformin (Walmart's price is $10 for a three- month supply) was difficult. Getting a medical furlough for a few hours to get the MRI for my shoulder turned into an eleven-month fight.

Then there was the craziness of the guards. On April 1, the counselor, Ms. Terry, was on a rampage about the appearance of the dorms. It was motivated by the upcoming regional review. One fellow described it as "they only care about how things look, not how this place is run." Part of the challenge is that one's entire "stuff" is supposed to fit into a 3' x 5' locker. It is especially difficult when there are extra clothes, legal work, etc.

They closed the chapel for a couple days to mop, wax, and buff the floors. It should have taken just a couple hours, but the work ethic was poor. The irony is that as bad as the inmates "work," their ethic is much higher than the staff!

I tried to estimate the number of hours I spent doing legal research and came up with approximately 1500. To pay attorney fees at the low rate of $200 per hour would have been $300,000 of billing. If I wasn't working on my own case, I was helping all those who asked. It certainly honed my legal research skills which I used extensively while there and in the succeeding years.

All during this time, Linda was carrying the load with the tax business. Since we could talk daily (but only ten minutes) we could pack any questions into that time. Plus, every trip here for visitation was also filled with tax conversation. Occasionally, she would mail me information to process, and then I would ship it back to her so she could input it into the computer.

On Special Assignment

Often my letters would include an interjection of OMIT! That stood for "One More Idiotic Time." There were many days when that was included several times. It's no wonder that the level of compliance with the "rules" was so low. Officers would make up new rules on the spot, and fail to keep the written ones. The next officer would negate the previous inconsistency and substitute his own.

One of the unusual things with which to contend was the assignment of various gay persons. This was especially true of those who had already had partial surgery or were taking hormones. I don't remember anyone discriminating against them. But that did not take away the weirdness when you saw someone standing at a urinal adjusting his bra.

One was nicknamed "Candy." Raymond hated the very sight of him/her and they would get into shouting matches. Apparently, one day Raymond called him the "N" word, and Candy fought him with the strength of a man and the viciousness of a female. Candy, too, had huge pent up anger and ripped Raymond's face apart. Reporting it would have been trouble for both, so Raymond made up a story that he had fallen into a pile of rocks and torn his face. He judiciously stayed out of sight from the officers until his face could heal. It was an overload of both testosterone and estrogen!

The story did reach the office and SIS came down to investigate. They even took Raymond to the hospital to see if the injuries need additional medical treatment. They put Raymond in the SHU (special holding unit) until they could arrange shipping to another facility.

One of the delights was to organize the Southern Gospel quartet, and have them sing in the chapel services. "Moses" was our lead singer, David sang the tenor and played the keyboard, I was the baritone, and Kerry sang the bass. All of us had previous quartet experience, and it was easy to blend. Whenever it was announced that the quartet would sing, the chapel would be packed with many standing in the back.

One of the deficiencies in medical care was the dental work. The dentist was scheduled to come two days a week, but often would skip two or three weeks. He refused to do any drilling or filling work. If you had a problem, he simply wanted to pull the tooth. In our dorm, Ricky's pain was great, so he allowed him to pull a tooth. The dentist was so rough that he broke the bone getting it out and cracked the tooth next to the one he pulled. Ricky went to bed for two days to heal.

In April, I was put on the call-out sheet to see the optometrist. My "eye story" is a saga all its own. As a child getting ready to start kindergarten, I needed an eye exam. There was many "discoveries." I was blind in my left eye. Further analysis revealed that the blindness was not because the eye could not see, it was just "lazy." The medical name is amblyopia. I was required to wear a patch on my right eye at times to try to force that eye to begin working. Sight began to develop and in that eye, I was far-sighted, a condition known as hyperopia. The doctor also discovered that my left eye also had an unfinished lens. Looking with that eye would remind someone of looking through early kinds of glass where the vision is blurry. It's a condition that cannot be corrected with glasses.

Amblyopia also had a side effect of the eye being angled wrong, so that each eye acts independently of the other. Therefore, my brain must decide on which image it will accept at any moment. Therefore, I do not have stereo vision, a requirement to have depth perception. The answer is to learn to cope by using lateral comparisons.

My right eye was listed at 20/400. The technical name was myopia. The effect of that was I could not see the blackboard even sitting in the front row in the classroom. I was fitted with thick glasses. The doctor warned us that if my eyes worsened, I could easily become "legally blind." Imagine that news given to a five-year old.

But God had a different plan. I would get an eye exam about every two years. With each new prescription, the strength of the glasses would be reduced. That would continue throughout my life. In my early forties, I switched to contact lens and the healing process continued. When I entered the camp in Atlanta, obtaining the proper solutions for my contacts was very difficult. I had no need for the contacts, since seeing far away was not necessary. I simply quit wearing contacts altogether.

I was 60 when I entered the camp. Normally, by that time people are struggling with presbyopia. That usually is corrected by getting

On Special Assignment

"reading glasses" or bifocals. I had gone through a brief period when that was desirable.

When I went for my eye exam, my prescription had downgraded to just 20/40 in the left eye. I was outfitted with a new pair of government issued glasses (certainly not designer frames). Since I used them so sparingly, it didn't really matter.

There was a positive note from the exam. Because of the diabetic diagnosis, the doctor checked for any bleeding from the veins in the back of the eyeball. There were none. As a further note, seven years later my eyes are still healthy.

Today at age 70, I wear glasses for night-time driving. I still do not need reading glasses, able to read even 6-point type at close distances. Since there has been no surgeries or medicines, the Great Physician gets all the credit!

Visiting the PA in the medical office got me some sympathy, but he had no authority to write an order for me to get an MRI. I explained my pain that I would get after writing for little while. Since I was writing something several hours a day, it was a significant problem. I was finally able to get an appointment with the MD. After hearing the story, she agreed to write the order, but, of course, it still had to get approvals from administration. Fortunately, one of my friends, James, worked in the Warden's office and he spoke directly to the Warden about it. He shared that the Warden had given a positive response.

I was summoned to the counselor's office the last of April to sign the papers for a medical furlough to get the MRI. The date was May 12—only 3.5 months after the accident. The pressure put on by our congressman was successful. We knew of many others who had not received needed medical attention in years. We were very grateful.

Late in April, a man named Clay Harris "fell" out of top bunk, seriously injuring himself. After a couple days in the hospital, he passed away. It precipitated an official inquiry as to whether he had help "falling." It did result in an order that all beds were to be placed in side by side manner and not as bunks. I did not hear the end of the story as to whether his family ever sued the BOP, because he had a medical pass which required him to have a lower bunk. Such behavior was normal for the BOP.

Pastor Clarke was gone by the end of May and by default I was now "the pastor." Moving into that role garnered much more attention. Many with whom I had no personal relationship would address me, "Hi, pastor," as I would walk by. They would offer me food and other items. I simply continued to show them the love of Jesus.

Rather than become the "every week" speaker, I called my Bible school men together. There were about fifteen engaged in our weekly classes, but six were on a quest to answer the call to preach. I told them that I would still speak once or twice a month, but I wanted to further prepare them. They would be assigned a time to preach. They would prepare their sermon outline and review it with me prior to the event. After they preached, I would meet privately and give them a critique. Then at the next class, we would get feedback from all the guys. I wish I could convey to you the response. It was a divine moment. The diligence with which the men pursued their calling was amazing to watch.

Terry Woodard took the next public opportunity to explain to the chapel congregation this change in focus. While I wanted them to have the best preparation possible for when I departed the facility, I had a loftier goal. It was to teach the discipleship principle of multiplication. By modeling multiplication to them, hopefully it would produce a great harvest.

Every so often, guards would pull a "strip search" as we were leaving the visiting room. Tommy and I were the first two called. It was common practice for us the get various goodies from the visiting room such as packets of mayo, mustard, and tabasco to supplement out food in the dorms. Knowing this, I always hid them properly, so when I was called for the search, they found nothing. When I was given the okay to dress and leave, I picked up those condiments and took them to the dorm. It was another example of silly games.

If one of the chaplains on staff would not be available for each chapel service, they were expected to provide a visiting preacher for each service. It was hit and miss, and mostly miss. Sometimes we would be informed of someone or a group who were scheduled.

On Special Assignment

Often, they didn't show up. The other challenge was the quality of those who volunteered for this service. As an example, one day for the 1pm service on Sunday, a visitor arrived. There were only 14 men who showed up for the service. He thought he was in charge for everything including the music. One by one the men started to leave, and by the end there were only four left. When I met with the chaplain the following week, I suggested that he not get invited to return.

One of the men in our dorm had a heart attack and was taken to the hospital via ambulance. They discovered a blockage and were able to open the artery by inserting a stent. The day after he returned he was summoned to the admin office. There were no questions as to how he was doing, or even talk about his imminent release. They only wanted to know "how did your wife find out you were in the hospital?" He told them he didn't know—if someone had called her, he had no idea who it was. OMIT (One More Idiotic Thing)

It was always exciting when one of the men received their new study bible with their name engraved. For many, it was the first bible they had ever owned. For most, it was the nicest bible they had ever had for their own. They expressed their thanks to me, and some wrote the Stimacks a note of gratefulness. Julio was the first to receive one in Spanish and he was doubly grateful.

It seemed there was always special needs coming from the men's families. One day Richard, a black from Columbus GA who received news that his 39-year-old daughter was struck twice by vehicles on the interstate. They life-lined her to Grady hospital in Atlanta but they were short on other details. He and Earl came to my cube where we had a prayer session. Both of Richard's boys were in prison on drug issues, so they needed lots of prayer. Richard feels he's called to preach, but he has little background and was already 60 years old. Nevertheless, God is no respecter of age.

Larry Roundtree had arrived at Atlanta just a week before I did. On his initial medical evaluation, it was determined he needed a new set of false teeth. After 21 months, he received the new set of teeth. To his amazement, they actually fit!

God was moving mightily and the gospel was presented by our core disciples daily and at every opportunity. Men responded during the chapel services, but just as often salvation occurred in the dorms during the bible study groups. It was exciting to hear the testimonies of those coming to Christ. I would even schedule "salvation by appointment" when someone we had been cultivating the ground and sowing the seed was now ready to accept the invitation.

The bigger task was discipleship. Most men, even if they had some kind of Christian upbringing, had paid little attention to it. Many rejected all they had known when they surrendered to the drug culture. Accepting Christ in prison rarely gave them the discipleship training so vital to becoming a "life-long follower" of Christ. That is where God directed me to concentrate my activities for long-term results.

May 12 arrived and it was the day to get my MRI. The driver, Erik, came for me at 7:25am and as we were walking to the OIC office, they called a fire drill. We proceeded to get the furlough papers, and left through the administration building. Then we went to the main prison building up front and were checked out by a lieutenant. He glanced at the papers but mainly check my ID and then we were off to the South Fulton Hospital. We arrived at 8:10am. I checked in through admissions and then the driver left. I was taken down to the MRI department and sat alone for over an hour in a small waiting room (three chairs). I had taken a book to read and a couple of Sudoku puzzles.

This was my first ever MRI and it was interesting. The order was for two pictures, one with "contrast". I laid down on a small table which was moved into the machine. It was not for "claustrophobics." I just shut my eyes and dozed off a couple times. The technician gave me ear plugs to soften the noise. It took about 40 minutes total. I was taken back to the front door where a call was made to get a ride back. We stopped at the main building to get checked in by another lieutenant. There was one minor mishap in the process. I had left my ID card in my pocket during the MRI, so it erased the magnetic markings on the card which made for another challenge. They were able to re-enter the information but it was a hassle.

The driver was kind enough to ask the kitchen to make me a plate of food so I didn't miss lunch. They put aside a generous portion, so it served as two meals for me. I got acquainted with the driver on those trips. His story was typical. He was just a month from

On Special Assignment

leaving after having served over 17 years in prison. He never had a disciplinary write-up during that time. He had been a "town driver" for over a year. I'm still amazed at the prison system which killed his life from age 25 to 42. With his healthy attitude, I believe he will make it on the outside.

Erik had requested the twelve-month half-way house/home confinement program. The BOP routinely resisted applying the new law. He even had his sentencing judge, and his congressman write recommendations, and they were completely ignored.

Negotiating the phone system could be a real challenge. At times, I had to stand in line for it to become available. When it was, I would go through the codes necessary to place an outside call. The calls outside the Atlanta area cost 23 cents per minute. If for some reason, the call was dropped after connection, I had to wait for an hour to re-dial the call. Minutes were rationed at 300 minutes a month, and 400 during November and December.

We decided early on that most of my calls would be to Linda, and that she would then disseminate whatever information she wished. Occasionally, I would call my mother. I talked with Linda almost every day for about ten minutes, unless she was visiting. As with most things, we simply "made it work."

Week after week there would be needs to be addressed. A normal day could have between 20 and 30 men requesting counsel and/or prayer. One evening the Judge stopped me to share that his wife, Myrna, had a seizure at home, fell in the bathroom and lodged between the sink and tub. Their son was unable to free her and called 911. The fall also disconnected her oxygen. At the hospital, she was pronounced dead, but they tried one more time to shock her back to life and it worked. The Judge was distraught, and we immediately went to prayer. God brought peace to his heart. There was truly an answer to prayer as Myrna is still alive and doing well eight years after the fact.

One of the ironic happenings every week was the race to get the mattress of one who was leaving. Mattresses ranged from okay to horrible—too hard, too lumpy, too soft, etc. Upon arrival, men generally accepted the worse of the mattresses. Since we had a weekly turnover of ten men, mattresses were constantly moving even between dorms. Men would connive in different ways to retrieve a different mattress if it happened to be a little better.

The BOP would do special meals for various religious groups. There was no question that the Moslems were treated the best during Ramadan—with a special meal each night after sundown for 30 days. The Christians were given a special meal for Pentecost celebration.

One day in early June, one of my "preacher boys," Terry, organized a symbolic event to encourage changing of various laws and administrative rules for the benefit of the prisoners. He called this a "Jericho walk." He gathered as many as would participate (about forty men) to walk around the track seven times in silence. At the end, the entire group would gather and shout in faith that the walls would crumble down.

In the law library, I would get many coming to get counsel. On a low day, there would be five or six men seeking help. It could range from legal questions, to tax issues, to personal relationships, or spiritual discussions. On a busy day, there would be 25 or 30. With a population at the camp of about 500 men, and a turnover of ten per week, I came in contact with around 1500 men during my stay. I would venture to say that I counseled at least a third of those during my time there.

One of the young black men in my dorm was nicknamed, "Dirty." By his own admission, he had lived all his adult life destroying himself. His mother was a Christian and had prayed for him regularly. He was trying to do things better (he was 46 at the time). He accepted a Bible and began in earnest to listen to Jesus. I remarked to him one evening, "You'll be the first person called "Dirty" who has a clean heart," and he loved it.

A few nights later, Dirty (real name Marty Givens) came by my cube. He told me he had made complete peace with God. He expressed hope his mother would live long enough for him to get out of prison and see her. She's prayed for him all the years he was living a life of sin and crime. A friend had written to me that he was praying that Dirty would change his name to "Mr. Clean." He loved the idea.

On Special Assignment

My roommate, James, who had been incarcerated for over a decade had major issues with his teeth. He put in a request to see the dentist just to get a filling. After submitting numerous requests for over a year, he still had not been able to see the dentist even though he came to the camp twice a week. James' story was the norm.

If there was any quality that all the staff suffered from, it was laziness. Things that should have taken an hour would not get done for weeks. I finally cornered the counselor who was to have completed some paperwork for my transfer out. By policy it is supposed to be 17-19 months prior to release. Six months later it still was not done. Even when pressed, they would find some way around it.

When the law changed to allow up to twelve months of halfway house/home confinement (up from six months) nothing changed. The BOP was more concerned about keeping their population up because it was business. If the prison population declined many would lose their jobs. The union pressured the BOP to not release anyone early.

It was the same way with the courts. Men would file suit to be allowed the early time. The court would simply sit on the motion for months without any ruling, and thereby deny men the release the law allowed. And to think some still refer to it as a "justice" system.

The middle of June 2009 a short but powerful storm came through. It knocked the power out. Emergency generators kicked in and gave power for about 30 minutes. It knocked out the phones in the back dorms. In addition, the PA system was disabled. Since the PA system was used to alert men to visits, they employed "runners" to find men on the campus to tell them to report to the visitation room.

I noted on June 14, that it was my 700th day at the camp. Since I was considered a short timer, keeping track seemed to help the time pass. Had the BOP honored the new law, I would be leaving in less than 60 days. By then the nickname for the place was "Camp Cupcake" and that was kind.

When Eugene Carter received his Bible, he shared his excitement with me. A huge smile came on his face and he said, "It even had my name on it." Those little things paid huge dividends in the lives of those who had never had any luxuries previously.

Time continued to move along as I tried to get the medical help. On June 24, I received word from the counselor that I had been granted a medical furlough to see the orthopedic surgeon on July 13. Since most inmate requests are ignored, I figured that the intervention of our Congressman Young had helped. The counselor grumbled, "Well, I've got one of your things done for you."

It was July 6th before I was given the results of the MRI. It simply said, "there is a complete tear of the tendon, the supraspinatus muscle at its critical zone with a small amount of fluid seen within the subacomial and subdeltoid bursa." It also noted "significant degenerative change and inflammatory changes in the AC joint space." I had to get Doc Mike to interpret all that for me. He warned me that the healing process is generally slow, and that I really needed good therapy which was not available there at the camp.

The "entrance exam" was supposed to have included a TB test. I finally received it in June, almost two years after arriving there, and on July 6th I was informed the results were negative.

There was always rejoicing when one of the men would get their case "reversed and remanded." For Derek, it took nine years. Eugene received word that his sentence was reduced by 37 months. The BOP opposed every motion that would help the inmates. But everyone on the inside rejoiced for any victory.

It seemed like there was always some drama unfolding. The morning of July 13, we were informed that George in E Dorm passed away during the night. He was discovered by his roommate when he tried to wake him for breakfast. The weekend before, his wife came to visit and they sat right behind Linda and me. She was excited because he finally was willing to do puzzles with her. He was being treated for various health issues such as heart, sleep apnea, etc. There was no immediate indication as to the cause of death.

This was my morning to go see the orthopedic surgeon, Dr. John Keating. The officers were late so we left about 40 minutes behind

On Special Assignment

schedule, but they took me right in at the doctor's office. He wanted to do three more x-rays. After viewing all that, he believed he could do the whole thing arthroscopically which would involve cleaning the rotator cuff area, including scaping some build-up off the bone, and inserting a couple screws to help re-attach the tendon. I signed the paperwork to do the surgery. However, I had to wait for the BOP to actually schedule it. As you will see, that took another six months to work through the bureaucracy.

The rules allowed men to kiss their wives when they arrived in the visitor's room, and again when they left at the close of the day. Andrew was summoned to the Administrative Office and admonished about being too affectionate when his wife was leaving because they French-kissed. That one deserved another OMIT!

Judges now routinely order that everyone must have a DNA test before they can be released back into the population even though the law only requires it for sex offenders and murderers. It came my time to have the blood drawn for this test. The nurse who took the blood was very poor and poked me seven times to get enough blood.

Kary received an internal mail informing him that his administrative remedy request to the Regional Office was procedurally rejected because he didn't include a copy of the warden's rejection. However, the warden didn't send a written rejection. He let the request lapse by simply not responding within 30 days. By regulation that is a rejection. This just shows the games that BOP administration played to deny inmates their rights.

A fellow named Abe was found dead in his bed one morning. They, of course, removed his body to some morgue, but it was couple days before they notified his wife. They could not tell her where the body had been taken, and it took her three days calling the various funeral homes before she could locate the body. OMIT!

Another bit of irony for Abe was that two days after he died, he received notice he had won his appeal and would have been set free. It gave his wife cause to file a false imprisonment claim. Had he never come to prison, he might still be alive. Only God knows.

On Sunday, July 26, 2009 one of my "preacher boys," Andrew, who had been taking the bible school classes preached his first sermon in chapel. The general consensus was that he did well, and that he had great potential as a preacher.

That evening in the service we had special prayer for Moses and Billie Romera who were being released that week. Since Moses was the lead singer in our Southern Gospel quartet, we would have to find a replacement or disband that group.

One day as I was walking past the office, the counselor, Ms. Terry, called me in. She asked about my leaving date, and I informed her that the twelve-month date would be the following Monday. (Federal rules had been changed so that one could receive half-way house assignment and/or home confinement the last 12 months of a sentence. But the BOP fought that vociferously wanting to keep the population up. That whole subject needs another book to discuss it fully.) She suggested that she would work on a 9 or 10 months assignment. It turned out to be an empty promise.

Chris Kidwell had become an avid participant in the daily Bible study. He posed a question as to what character quality I thought would be the most important one we could teach our children. He offered his opinion that it should be "obedience." As a psychologist, he certainly had some good insights. I disagreed, saying the number one quality I would instill would be "gratefulness." I've seen too many kids who obeyed out of fear or duty, and missed the joy of life. When obedience is with "gritted teeth" character suffers. But a child who is grateful, is fairly easy to guide in obedience. We had so many examples in those who were confined, that the truth of gratefulness was compelling.

Men were often their own worst enemy. A Hispanic man from Texas joined me on my evening walk in order to talk. In the six laps (1.5 miles) he poured out his heart. He had received notice from his wife that she was filing for divorce. He listed the reasons such as his controlling, manipulative and angry manner. He acknowledged that all of it was true. Even being in prison for thirty months, he was still running her life, or at least trying to do so. They had been married for 22 years and had three young children. I explained the only thing under his control now was himself, and he needed to accept the challenge that his main goal would to become pleasing to God. I regret that I did not have enough time with him to mentor him to relational health, but I was able to point the way.

It was a special joy to see the various men who received their bibles from the Stimacks. I would run into them in various places such as the serving line in the dining hall. Demetri had an ear-to-ear smile and it expressed the thrill in his heart at receiving his personalized study Bible.

Crescenco came again to walk so he could talk. With another six laps, he discussed his admitted issues: selfishness, jealousy, manipulation, control of others, self-pity and insecurity. I began working on scriptural projects that would address each of these issues. He was hoping that improving in these areas would help save his marriage, but I could not promise him. I did assure him it would improve his relationship with God, especially if he actually practiced the scriptures he was learning.

A fellow in another dorm who knew Crescenco well, saw that I had spent some time with him. After Crescenco left, this fellow came and said to me "There will be a special place in heaven for guys like you who can deal with men like him without going crazy." But God continued to give "extra grace."

On my August 5, 2009 notes, I wrote that the "homiletics" class had gone well. The assignment for that evening was to develop a 3-point outline using alliteration. One fellow did exceptionally well. The next assignment was to do double alliteration—i.e., all sub-points had to be alliterated as well. I was so impressed with the spirit of co-operation and support between the men.

August 16, 2009 was a time of great conversation with Linda. It was just a day before our 41st anniversary. I was the first one called to the visitor's room that morning. Before I went, I had written my 365th devotional, and those are now published in the book, Refined Through Suffering. I had arranged through the gentleman who supplied all the vending items for the visitor's room that he would get a small anniversary cake for Linda and me.

Bob Bedford

Here's my anniversary note to Linda: **Happy Anniversary**

My dearest Linda,

Today, 41 years ago, we exchanged vows in the old Asbury Bible Church. We promised "for better or worse, richer or poorer, in sickness and in health" to be married. I think we've had a lot in each category.

Today, I give thanks to God for you and think of these specific things.

You've had to manage the tax business virtually on your own, but you've amazed the worse skeptics. You've served as press secretary, mail clerk, national traveler, and publisher. You've expanded your hospitality gifts to a whole new world of inmate families, and even endeared yourself to prisoners you've never met. You've survived a major catastrophe on your leg and seem to be stronger for it.

You've seized opportunities to reconnect with old friends and made dozens of new ones by your personal interest in them you so often convey. We've found ways to develop new levels of intimacy, to maximize communication in a ten-minute call, and share our unity in a six-hour face to face time with no cell phones to interrupt! Our shared time in doing puzzles has given us a lot of enjoyment.

Our future is great as we continue to learn how to appreciate our irreconcilable differences and trust God to make us one in Him.

I love and cherish you, Bob

That evening we had a great service. Kary was the MC, and I gave a devotional from Psalm 119:161, "I'm in awe of God's Word." Then Karsten preached, and I observed how well he was improved. That was important because the following year, he was "promoted" to the senior pastor in charge of the chapel. He remained there until January 2017.

One of the frustrating issues was the unwillingness for the staff do their assigned work. The laws had been changed so that inmates could receive twelve months of half-way house/home confinement. I had been working for some time to get the counselor to write up the recommendation since I was now less than twelve months. I was aware of another inmate who had been recommended for the twelve months and it had been approved by the warden.

On Special Assignment

I was finally summoned to the office to discuss this paperwork. In the conversation, I made him aware of the gentleman who had received the recommendation. He wanted proof. I refused and told him that I did not trust him. The information was available to him through other means. He then wanted to know if I was going to file a lawsuit which would name him. If I filed a suit, then he would not work on the paperwork. I responded to him, "I have not, but you make it awfully tempting." He thanked me for my honesty. The men in our main bible study group promised to back me even if it meant they would be disadvantaged.

I noted that three men had received their requested study bibles. Santana (one of the preacher boys) has been struggling to learn sermonizing and he stayed and read the "helps" section for several hours. Larry had received his "large print" and read more scripture than he had in several years. Sergio saw me on the track and expressed his deep appreciation for the gift. So a black, a Caucasian, and a Hispanic all received their bibles the same day—it was truly a multicultural ministry.

Occasionally, I would experience the feeling of loneliness. The means of communication in our current culture require phones and internet and both were banned. While my family and friends were supportive and I received more communications than any of the other 500 men in that inmate population, so many other things were happening on the outside that I simply had no way of knowing. It gave a feeling of being "cut off." I often had to address the loneliness issue with other men there.

Day after day I continued to walk laps—usually 4-5 miles a day. There were many laps in which I was counseling someone. When I wasn't counseling, I was reading a book, which I could do without stumbling or running into someone in spite of the condition of the track.

Early in September I noted that Officer Parsons called a census (senseless) count because he was on the warpath. He had intercepted contraband which included a significant amount of small alcohol bottles and about twenty cartons of cigarettes. His timing was way off because it was just before those who had jobs outside the fence were returning to the camp. He couldn't get the population stabilized, so he never made the count. OMIT!

It was birthday time again and the cards began pouring in. Sometime ten or more a day. Parson used to have each person quote his registration number for each piece of mail. But getting this much mail was a nuisance for him so he allowed me to just say it once. I think my record was 18 pieces of mail in a single day.

For my "birthday" supper, it took a bowl of pasta that my roommate had fixed and added hot sauce, oysters and squeeze cheese. The things we counted as "special" must be understood in the context of those circumstances.

Every so often, the camp administrator would call a "town meeting." Usually, it was to explain some new policy or procedure. The one this month was to beg the inmates to conform to the rules, particularly not bringing in contraband. By repeating himself three times, his speech lasted 5 minutes. Had the staff all practiced doing "the right thing," the inmates would have probably followed suit. As it was, they just laughed at the staff. OMIT!

Having available time meant that I could prepare study material. My daughter, Sandi, asked for lessons for a youth camp. Linda asked for lessons for the upcoming Camp Meeting Kids Reunion. It not only helped me stay current in my learning and preparing mode, but it was ministry beyond the camp.

There were frequent maintenance issues. The one in September was the hot water heater in the kitchen quite working. As is the general case, no repair could be done quickly. That necessitated them using Styrofoam plates and cups. It took a week for the kitchen to be back in full mode.

One of the disappointments is not being able to celebrate birthdays with family members. September 11 was Kamen's 11th birthday. Another is having loved ones pass away. Linda was in Indiana and visiting her dad when we had our daily call. She handed the phone to him and I was able to talk with him for a few minutes. We had no idea that would be my last time to talk with him—he passed away a few days later on October 1.

Another gay person was admitted and assigned to C dorm. There was so much controversy that they moved him to B dorm so that his

On Special Assignment

cube would be just a few feet from the officer's desks. It lessened the outbreaks but the feelings ran deep. It was a tug of war. OMIT!

I was always amazed at the access to "contraband." One evening I observed the man across from me carrying in a black duffle bag. As I watched, he took out a significant number of Heineken beer cans and put them into a bucket with ice. I had no idea when they were going to have their beer party. Even though that is risky behavior, they persisted anyway. I wasn't around to even see the party.

There was a changing of the guards every three months. For this quarter, we were assigned some decent ones. They let it be known that "as long as you don't mess up my counts, I'll leave you alone: no shake downs, no extra counts, etc. But mess that up, and I'll play 'bad cop'."

Some guards made up their own rules. Officer Kane was a real nut case—control was his mantra. He required everyone eating supper to go out a different door from the one they entered or he would assign you "extra duty." But no one knew the rule until they violated it. No other officer in the whole system had such a rule. OMIT!

One night they did the regular 8p count. This was the only camp in the nation that does an 8p count. They cleared it about 8:30p and then called another one at 8:55p. Then they had the regular count at 10p. It was such that the absurd became "normal." OMIT!

Joe Pogue was a classy gentleman from the southern part of Georgia. He served in Vietnam and his life was spared when a young white soldier smothered a grenade with body to protect everyone else. Joe wrote a commendation for a Medal of Honor and gave a speech of gratefulness at the ceremony when the medal was presented to his parents. He still gets emotional telling the story—the young man is #156 on the Viet Nam Memorial.

Several of the men asked about having communion. The assistant chaplain was Anglican and so he was reticent to let anyone who was not ordained to administer the elements. But he readily gave me the elements to have communion anytime I wanted to celebrate. Announcing communion always seem to pack out the chapel.

I continued dealing with the government (especially the IRS) throughout my time there. Sam received an objection from the government in dropping his Tax Court suit. One can only go to the Tax Court with an issue if a Notice of Deficiency was issued. In his case, the IRS negated his Notice. That meant the Tax Court no longer had jurisdiction, and the government objected! OMIT! He also received a notice that his claim for a 2002 refund was denied, even when he had not filed a claim.

It was always encouraging for me to have my "preacher boys" hungry for additional learning. In addition to the regular group classes, several wanted extra mentoring. Karsten was one of those and he was on a fast track to ordination. Terry was another one and I was always glad to adjust my schedule to spend time with each one.

I noted that on October 13 it was "wedding day." Men were allowed to get married with special permission and the chaplain would perform the ceremonies. On this day, there were five men from the camp who were married and fifteen men from the adjacent medium security prison also married. Those in the camp usually had a projected "out date" to look forward to, but those from the prison often were long-termers.

One of the daily challenges was to get enough good nutrition, especially for a diabetic. High starch items were normal. I noted this month that the mashed potatoes had roach parts all through them. The meats often had a rotten odor. I took significant advantage of the fresh fruit that was available. While it was "against the policy" of the institution to export food from the dining hall, I did so out of necessity. Others would give me their apples and oranges but I usually had to barter for bananas. Survival was the goal. I could not get enough quality food to gain any weight.

We continued to hammer the administration to adjust to the new law that allowed up to twelve month's half-way house and home confinement. The BOP was totally resistant to the idea, and found every conceivable way to block it from happening. Keeping the prison population high is job security for them. I filed suit and the judge ordered the BOP to respond. But as was very usual, the case sat on the judge's desk with no decision until the time frame ran out and the motion was moot.

On Special Assignment

The control of the food supply was atrocious. Most of the fresh vegetables were stolen from the warehouse by those who worked there and then sold on the "black market" to enrich themselves. On this particular day, the menu called for chicken fajitas. But the onions, peppers, and tomatoes were stolen, so they cooked the chicken with cabbage—I wasn't sure what to label that!

In October, two additional men came to E dorm—one was a Buddhist and the other a Hindu. They often came to talk and I was able to give guidance in a number of areas. They became friends, and would come to chapel if they knew I was speaking. When I was nearing the time to leave, these two organized a going away party for me. No one there had ever known of anyone having such a party. The creativity was demonstrated as they prepared pizza and several other items for the occasion. We estimate that over 100 men came for the party. And the crowd also included Moslems, Wiccans, Jews, and at least a dozen Christian denominations.

Chaplain Ray showed up for the 1p chapel service. I led the hymns he requested. He had brought elements to offer communion for both that service and the evening time of the next week. We could announce it all week to gain maximum attendance. Chaplain Ray was always respectful and helpful in administering the chapel.

I had gone to take a nap and slept for 25 minutes when James woke with the announcement that SIS (security) was there to shake down our dorm. There were two ladies this time. As one of them was getting ready to pat me down, she noticed my name, and said, "Bedford, oh you're the one who gets so much mail." I acknowledged that I did, and she followed up with, "And you go home soon." I didn't recall having ever seen her before but she obviously knew who I was.

I continued to work with my lead preacher boys on administrative issues. Learning how to schedule everyone who wanted to participate in the chapel ministry was just one of the functions. Teaching them how to lead the communion service was also important.

Satan is never happy when hearts are in unison. So a disagreement arose between a couple of the men regarding Fantasy Football.

I still don't understand all those "ins and outs" but I did have to mediate. We did finally mend hearts and the ministry continued forward.

A new fellow named Jeff came to our dorm and we developed a great friendship. He was thankful for my encouragement, and responded by fixing chef salads on several evenings. His wife was a fabulous smuggler and would smoke a pork roast and bring it in. A two-pound roast would provide enough meat for several salads.

"Slow" and "stop" properly described the movement to receive medical treatment. I had made a request on Sept 28 to get the surgery I needed for the rotator cuff injury. A written answer was date stamped Oct 23, but I did not receive it until Nov 16. All the communications were "in house." The slowness of the BOP administration was endemic. OMIT! The actual appointment with the doctor did not occur until December 11 and it would still be another six weeks before the surgery.

The chapel services sometimes had speakers from the outside who had been scheduled by the BOP chaplain. More often than not, the quality of preaching was not great. I figured that many were those who had no other venue offered to them, so they made themselves available to the prison. I noted that on Nov 22 that "the outside preacher went on for almost an hour, and if he had a "theme, outline, or plan" I could not detect it. He did have occasional volume—otherwise, sleep would have overtaken us.

Thanksgiving Day 2009 the BOP served a holiday meal. I received three slices of turkey, two slices of ham, a baked sweet potato, cornbread dressing and gravy. Dessert was custard pie and double-crusted apple pie. It was all good, but the quantity was so great I "exported" over half of it to eat later. That evening was our Gospel Concert night and various groups sang past 7:30p. The chapel was packed and we all concluded it had been a "good time."

Linda continued to minister to family members of the inmates. My roommate's mother was one of those. James told me how much his mom liked Linda and went on to say that she was the first "white" woman she had ever trusted. She grew up in Alabama amid some intense discrimination and had never developed a close

On Special Assignment

relationship with another white female. We continue to count James and his mother as family.

Often, I would go to Sam's cubicle to talk. He was a great lover of M&M's so he would insist that I have some. With my sugar issues, that was not on my list of foods. But to confirm our friendship, I would always take two of them. Gradually, I worked up to taking three.

One of the facts of prison life is the longer one is there the fewer the contacts with the outside world—either with visits or by mail. My life was a notable exception as I received more mail than any of the other 500 inmates. I sent out a plea to our friends that they would communicate with cards and letters to those in my friendship circle. Many responded and it made an incredible difference in the lives of the recipients. For some it was the first mail received in over five years. The command of Hebrews 13:3 is "Remembering the prisoners, as though you were in prison with them……….'

The BOP did provide a Christmas package each year. It consisted mostly of junk food, but, at least, it was token of "giving." Naturally, all religions represented were most happy to receive their Christmas gift. Christians have always been the ones to lead the world in giving, as taught by Jesus himself! Chaplain Ray worked with me to provide a Christmas Day service. We sang Christmas carols and Chaplain Ray brought the homily. Then I assisted him in serving communion. The crowd was somewhat small, but God's presence was real.

Meanwhile, my "pastor" classes continued and all 15 men were good students, but Karsten was the most intense in studying and applying the lessons. All of them seem to struggle with creating an expository outline, primarily trying to "stay within the text." I continued to teach them studying techniques to understand the context and reference points.

Men continued to file lawsuits to get the BOP to work with the law, but they resisted at all points, and the (corrupt) judges usually sided with the BOP. As an example, Jabari brought his decision on his 2241 filing to me to review and the judge's ruling echoed his assertion that he was a model prisoner. Therefore, he didn't need more than six months halfway house/home confinement.

The question we were left asking was "had he been a bad prisoner, would that have gained him more time in the program?" OMIT! It was clear how out of control both the administration and the judicial branches currently are.

One of the men wrote a play and he directed it in the chapel on Christmas Eve. It was about an hour long, and Andrew played the "preacher" in it. It was a great presentation especially considering the venue!

The Christmas lunch was a Cornish hen and sliced roast beef, cornbread dressing and pecan pie. The quantity of food was too much and much of it was exported to my cube for eating later.

The outside chapel speakers were rarely good. I noted that, in spite of getting new padded seating for the chapel, good seats could not make a poor service great. Various speakers had their own agenda and the focus was rarely on how the Word or the Spirit could elevate the men's character or spiritual development.

An interesting twist of how to manage around the system was the ability to do various kinds of work for other inmates. I often would be "contracted" to write a legal motion or brief, challenge an assessment for taxes, and address many other types of issues. Quite often it was done "pro bono" but occasionally men were able to compensate. They sometimes paid in the local currency ("macs") or they would have a relative deposit money into my commissary account.

I noted on December 31 that it was my 900th day of confinement. As 2009 ended, my thoughts were all on gaining my "freedom." It is very hard to describe the emotions of being almost there. But God's grace had been sufficient, and looking forward was my focus.

I had spent very little time playing games, but Bill from South Louisiana had bugged me to play chess. On January 1, I agreed to play. I had not played in twenty years, and I made a foolish move in the early stages that cost me the game. He wanted to play another game. He went on the attack quickly but left an unguarded man, so I was able to checkmate him without him being aware I was moving that direction. So the skills returned, and I left a champion.

On Special Assignment

January 10 was a milestone day. It was the day set for the ordination of Karsten Brinson, my star student in our local bible school. Linda had sent in an ordination certificate. I read, from the Discipline, the questions we asked of all candidates for ordination. He was able to answer firmly and with conviction. We had two outside ministers in that evening, and we invited them to participate. Others also gathered in and laid hands on Karsten. The Holy Spirit was there in an incredible way, and sealed that night. He truly was ordained by God, and carried on ministry until January 2017—seven years longer there in the Atlanta camp, and now in the Atlanta community.

A friend (who at the time worked for the BOP) meanwhile was advocating for me to get released. He secured the date of Feb 8, and we began working toward that time. When I first heard the date, I had difficulty believing it because of the callousness of the BOP and the courts.

A few days later I was paged to the office expecting to get more information on leaving. That meeting was simply to sign the papers for the medical furlough papers to receive the long-awaited rotator cuff surgery. Mr. Masters told me to see the secretary, Mrs. Smith, the next week to finalize transportation to the halfway house. He was not kind enough to even confirm my leaving date.

January 17 was set for me to preach my final chapel service. The chapel was full. The choir had some very special music. My message that evening was titled, "Defining Moments" based on the story of Elijah and Elisha from II Kings 2-3. The three points were, A Divine Appointment, A Divine Intersection and Divine Opportunity. I had taken a white hand towel to use as my "mantle." When I got to the point of Elijah leaving, I threw the "mantle" down on the floor and made the point someone would have to pick it up when the prophet was gone. The towel had landed close to Karsten Brinson, who we had just ordained the week before. It truly was a "divine moment" where the Holy Spirit's presence was real. When he reached down and picked it up, applause broke out all over the crowd and many were in tears. Karsten asked if he could keep it and, of course, he did.

The next day, I kept hearing all over the campus about the message the previous night. Some called it the best sermon they had ever heard, but it was the Spirit who made it so. Everyone who was there had been deeply moved. Robert Granda stopped by the library to tell me how much the message had impacted him. He said he had already discussed it with 30 men that day, and he had also shared it with his wife.

When I went to see the secretary about my leaving, she was shocked that Mr. Masters had not given me the date. She confirmed the date and then asked what would be my transportation to Tampa. If I could not make arrangements, I would be transported via the BOP bus which would require me to handcuffed and shackled for what would be at least 8 hours. That was motivation enough to get alternative travel. Linda was able to set schedule so that she would transport me.

On January 22, I was paged to the administration building. The administrator informed me the surgery was too close to my exit date, and I had to choose one or the other because there would not be time to do the post-surgery rehabilitation. I reminded him there was no rehab available at the camp and I would have to do the rehab on my own. I had already discussed that with the orthopedic doctor. (That would prove to be a very prophetic statement.) The administrator got back on the phone with the prison doctor and got both dates approved.

That same day Officer Parsons came to our bible study to round up people for the breathalyzer test and all of us were to report. Of course, there was laughter because I and all the other men strictly obeyed the rules. Parsons knew that we would all pass so he wouldn't have to do any follow-up work. OMIT!

Then the day came for me to have the first surgery.

Medical Story of Rotator Cuff Surgery

Earlier in the book, I told of falling while playing racquetball, and tearing the tendon in my right shoulder. I was unable to get immediate help, and the BOP kept delaying getting corrective surgery. After exhausting every avenue we had within the BOP, we turned to our Congressman. Linda was able to gain the attention of Mr. Young. He had been in Congress for a long time and had significant influence. He began putting the pressure on the BOP for me.

Finally, fifty-one (51) weeks after the injury I was scheduled for surgery. I was released to the Atlanta Medical Center and was transported there at 6a on Tuesday, January 26, 2010 They projected surgery time for 10a so I was prepped for the surgery soon after arriving at the hospital. It was estimated that the surgery would last less than an hour and with recuperation observation, I would be ready to return to the facility by late afternoon.

Ten o'clock came and went and I lay in the waiting area. Finally, a nurse came to inform me that there had been a couple of accidents where people required immediate surgery and so my case was delayed. They reported back around noon that there had been additional cases that needed the orthopedist's attention and that my time would be delayed until late afternoon. Of course, with imminent surgery, I was not allowed to have any food.

Four o'clock came and the nurse came to further delay my time. She asked if I would rather go, and come back another day. Since I had waited 51 weeks for this surgery, I was not about to leave without getting the work done. Finally, at 9pm I was taken to the surgery room, and Dr John Keating performed the corrective surgery. (Dr Keating is well known in the Atlanta Metro area as able to "fix" most any orthopedic problem.) It went well, but because of the late hour, I was admitted so I could spend the night. I rested fine, and was released back to the camp late morning on Wednesday.

However, this was just the beginning of a story, not the end.

Medical Story of Heart Surgery

January 29, 2010

God intervenes in unusual ways at times. I have my own analysis as to why my blood vessels went from clean to 100% blocked in that 30-month period. Since my rotator cuff surgery had been delayed for so long, the triggers of heart pain may not have happened timely. There is no doubt in my mind that even the medical personnel who did the surgery had no reason to talk about heart issues. My previous heart attack had been eleven years ago and I had had no new symptoms during that period. But the surgery was a major event and apparently triggered the heart pain.

12:30am. I awoke after sleeping for two hours with an ache in my left elbow and up a few inches on my upper arm. I went to the bathroom and decided to read for an hour. After reading, I laid down again but was unable to go back to sleep. I thought I had slept on it wrong as I had had similar type of paid in the past.

At 3am, I got back up and Danny McC saw me walking back to the microwave room and followed me in. He asked if I needed anything and I asked him for some pain medicine. With just having rotator cuff surgery on Tuesday evening, I was not yet back on my aspirin regiment. He had some capsules and I took a couple and read for another hour giving time for the pain medication to work. The medication did not work, but I returned to bed at 4am and tried to get some sleep, but none would come.

As I reflected on the pain, my mind went back ten years to July 29, 1999 when I suffered a heart attack while visiting in Alaska. Even though the pain was in a different location this time, it had a remarkable similarity to the pain I had with the heart attack. While I had been faithful to daily exercise, I knew I had not been able to get back to full strength physically. So I arose and went to find one of my doctor friends in the camp so I could get some medical advice.

Dr. Mike was in the shower but I found Dr. Billy. Dr. Billy was a retired family doctor from Mississippi and had his own medical issues. I discussed the symptom I was having and he confirmed my suspicions that it was probably a heart problem. As soon as Dr. Mike became available, he suggested I get immediate medical help.

On Special Assignment

Dr. Billy went with me to the OIC office and explained what was happening. They responded immediately by calling for the physician's assistant to come and they also called for an ambulance. The PA arrived shortly and we walked over to the medical clinic to await the arrival of the EMT's. I took a couple nitroglycerin tablets while I was waiting.

When the EMT's arrived, they stuffed both aspirin and more nitroglycerin into my mouth. They checked my vital signs and I was not overly stressed, but the pain persisted. They started an IV drip, transferred me to a gurney, and put me in the ambulance. They decided that my shirts (two t-shirts and a regular shirt) needed to be removed. But with all the wiring (EKG, IV's, etc.) the nurse simply grabbed scissors and began cutting them off. A BOP officer accompanied us to the Atlanta Medical Center again, and remained with me until the middle of the afternoon.

At the hospital, I was immediately processed in and had the obligatory tests. The evaluation was extensive. Around 10am, the decision was made to do a heart catherization and they scheduled it for 11:30am. Dr. Douglas, a noted cardiologist was scheduled for the procedure.

The Atlanta Medical Center had just opened a state-of-the-art renovated room to do heart catherizations. The electronics presented razor sharp images. Dr. Douglas applied the local anesthetic to my groin and I relaxed and slept through the entire procedure. I woke up and the doctor showed me the final composite picture which identified several blockages. He told me he would come the next day and discuss the details and possible procedures.

I was subsequently transferred to the CVCU (cardiovascular care unit). I was hooked up to all kinds of monitors. Each nurse is only assigned to two patients there and they worked twelve hour shifts. My request to inform Linda of the day's events was passed along to the evening nurse. Finally, a nurse put the call through on her cell phone and I was able to bring Linda up to date on all the events and to relieve her anxiety on what was going on. The network of inmate families had alerted her to the hospital trip but until I called she didn't know any more. After a day of no food, I was brought some supper (from the 1800 calorie per day diet)

All the vital signs were stable throughout the evening. In spite of my dislike of just lying in a bed for hours, I was able to get some sleep. There was light and noise, but after living that way for the past thirty months, it wasn't a major obstacle to getting some rest. Sleep was frustrated by the blood pressure machine taking a reading every fifteen minutes around the clock.

Dr. Douglas came early on Saturday morning on his rounds and had brought with him a drawing of my heart showing the locations of the blockages. Two of the heart arteries were 100% occluded, but in both cases the heart had created its own bypasses around the blockages. Through my faithfulness to exercise, particularly my walking about 25 miles a week, those small bypasses contributed to me not having another heart attack. Other blockages ranged from 40% to 80%. We talked through the options, and immediate surgery was not deemed critical, although he said it was the best option.

In view of my imminent return to Florida, he agreed to transfer his findings and recommendations to my cardiologist there for future considerations. The current plan would be to stabilize the condition with available drugs so I can make the trip and be functional for the foreseeable future.

Had I been at the camp that Saturday, it was visiting day and Linda would have come and discovered I wasn't there. The history of the BOP has been non-communication to inmate's families during medical crises. (They had even waited three days to notify one family of the death of the inmate.) While the rules permit families to visit at the hospital, the bureaucracy is so multi-layered it is considered a miracle to get a positive answer. It took over an hour, with multiple phone calls and paperwork, but permission was obtained and Linda made her way to the AMC—it was great to see her walking in that day.

As a follow-up on the escort from the BOP, anyone who leaves the facility must be constantly escorted unless they have received a "furlough." My previous trips to hospitals or doctors were arranged weeks in advance so there was always time to get the paperwork done—usually requiring 8-10 signatures. Since this was an emergency, no paperwork had been prepared. The officer assigned sat near during the ER room, then just outside the OR while the heart cath was in process. When I was transferred to the CVCU, he came and parked himself on a chair in the corner of the room. At approximately 3pm, Mr. Wilson, a case manager at the camp, came in and had medical furlough papers filled out and only needed my signature to complete. As soon as I signed them, he told the officer, Mr. Bates, he was no longer needed. Mr. Wilson's comment to me was to get well quickly so I could keep my February 8 departure date.

Since I was in an intensive care unit, visitation rules were 15 minutes every two hours. But Reggie, the day-time nurse, told Linda she could stay and she stayed till about 2pm. It allowed me to fill in other details that I had not previously shared. By then, I was on a heparin drip to thin my blood for approximately the 48 hours I was "caged" in the CVCU. Then about 2:30pm, the duty officer who had okayed Linda's visit also came to check on me and to make sure she had found her way and had secured her visit.

Another surprise was the chaplain coming to visit and he brought a greeting from my brother-in-law's family. (We had a great conversation about peace in difficult times.) The greeting came via the hospital's online service.

The balance of Saturday was routine. I was just uncomfortable lying in a bed all day. In addition to my restlessness, the food had been scant and tasteless. No fat, no salt, low carb, and no seasonings make the little bit of food very bland. So I was tired and hungry, but it was a situation I had to accept for the moment. Linda did return in the evening Saturday, but did not stay real long for they were holding to the posted schedules a little tighter. We learned that the doctor had okayed a move to a less intense level of care but no rooms were currently available so I was destined to spend another night in the CVCU.

There was a time on Friday morning right after I was transferred to the CVCU that I was close to being overcome with emotion. Coming to the end of this long ordeal of injustice, with just eleven days to go before release, I had envisioned a short transition and jumping back in the "saddle." The news from the cardiologist had many implications and I was just beginning to sort through them. The worst-case scenario was I was "at risk" for major dysfunction, if not death. And a best-case scenario had not been formulated. As tears began to well up in my eyes, I had to recommit the future to a loving God. In just a few minutes, the peace of God flooded my heart.

Sunday dawned and I had another tasteless breakfast—scrambled egg substitute, white grits, and one slice of white toast. No salt or other seasonings except pepper. Linda returned mid-morning and we learned that I was going to be transferred to a private room.

Nurse Reggie came in to tell us it was moving time and Linda helped with the moving, carrying my clothes, etc. It was a nice private room on the fourth floor overlooking the parking garage and emergency entrance. Even though it was only 1.5 hours before Linda would head north, it was the first "alone" time we've had in 30 months. We took time for some prayer, with great thanksgiving.

After Linda headed north, her brother Tim and his wife, Susan, came for a visit. Susan is so thoughtful and brought me a variety of fruit. Included was a big "baggie" of mixed fruit—melon, strawberries, blueberries, mango, and kiwi. It was delectable, I ate it all while they were there. Included also was a pound bag of pistachios, other fresh fruit, a little bit of dark chocolate and some reading materials and word and number puzzles.

The private room afforded me a phone so I was able to talk to all four of my daughters and some of the grandkids as well as several friends. This was truly a luxury! As Linda moved up the highway and then into the evening, we talked every hour or two till around 11pm.

There were lots of variables which contributed to a sleepless night. When the nurse came in she said they were going to give me blood pressure medicine. My B/P without medication has been running about 120/75 which I thought was excellent. But the cardiologist thought it should be lower to protect my heart. I was given two medicines plus a nitro-patch. Within an hour, my BP had fallen to 70/40 and that sent off all kinds of alarms. It took almost eight hours to get it back to 91/60.

In the middle of the afternoon I was informed there were plumbing problems in that room and they were moving me to another room with a view of Atlanta's downtown skyscrapers. Situated in the new room, the phone calls continued into the evening. Dr. Edwards appeared and indicated he was checking on me. He represented a medical review panel for the BOP and they had talked to the cardiologist, Dr. Douglas. He only stayed a few minutes and then was gone.

I had significant edema in my legs and that made it very difficult to sleep. The staff simply ignored that. I estimate that I only slept about two hours that night. I was given a reduced dose of blood pressure medicine but it quickly took my pressure down to 75/60. I received the prompt attention of the medical personnel. Finally, after another day of figuring out how little dosage I needed, they settled on the lowest dosage made.

With the blood pressure issue settled, I was released back to the camp on Wednesday. It was an exciting time for me because I was scheduled to be released to a half-way house the following Monday. After 908 days, it would be fabulous to breathe limited freedom. Little did I realize that there was another huge mountain to climb.

Back at the camp, I began in earnest to say all the "goodbyes" while at the same time working with the camp officials to have an unfettered release. On Friday, I was called in and informed that the BOP was unwilling to send me home with the heart condition. Instead of going home, I would be returning to the Atlanta Medical Center for open heart surgery. I even tried to convince them that I would take full responsibility for my health including the cost. They wouldn't budge. Calling Linda to inform her of the decision was a very difficult moment for both of us. In retrospect, God was providentially working through the BOP because they would pay for the entire process. So on February 9, after just seven days at the camp, I entered the hospital again.

The By-pass Surgery Story

The plan was to do four by-passes on February 11 and have me recuperate for 5-7 days. Two arteries were blocked 100%, one 85% and one 65%. They began prepping me on Wednesday evening for the 9am surgery on Thursday morning. Unfortunately, I do not remember much of the details of that day. They had scheduled the surgery with a renowned heart surgeon, originally from Nigeria. He did an excellent job (based on the succeeding years) and I am grateful. After a 4-hour surgery, I was put into the CVCU. Anyone who has been through similar surgery understands the annoyances of all the breathing tubes, IV's and monitors. But I progressed well and after just 24 hours, I was moved to a private room on the cardiac floor.

The usual times I was in hospital rooms was to visit others. My only other hospital experience prior to January 2010 was two days to set a broken arm when I was eight. I did not enjoy being in the hospital (except it was an upgrade from the camp!) After surgery, one needed item is rest. Hospital personnel show little regard for good sleep time. All the noise, and turning on lights, not to mention monitoring the blood pressure, and other vital signs only allowed for snatches of sleep. Complicating the heart surgery was my diabetic condition.

I had been on oral medication for the high sugar, but surgery demanded I go on insulin injections. I was very sensitive to the insulin, and they overdosed it frequently. While I have no symptoms with high sugar readings, low blood sugar produces a violent reaction. My blood sugar would fall to 40, producing chills, sweating, and tremors. It was not pleasant. The nurses would rush to get me orange juice to get the blood sugar up quickly.

By the following Monday, while the numbers for the heart and its functions was progressing well, other things began to go wrong. They had put a pressure sock on my right leg where they had stripped the vein for the by-passes. I learned later that it should have been changed daily. I began to experience pain in my lower right leg. A week after the surgery the sock was removed for the first time. Staph infection had invaded my leg and it was deep red from just below my knee down past the ankle.

Dealing with the infection was another routine. First, they needed blood samples to determine exactly what the specific type of strain of infection it was so that a special antibiotic could be prescribed. The infectious disease doctor appeared and explained what they would be doing. For the next 14 days, I would be giving three to five vials of blood five times a day. My veins tired and they began to look for new spots to prick to draw the blood.

Once the infectious disease doctor made a determination of the antibiotic, they placed it in an IV so it could drip 24 hours a day. I began to respond slowly. The pain in my leg was severe so that I could not place any weight on it. That doctor returned daily to check on my response to the medicine. I should have been walking as a therapy by then but it was out of the question. It was all I could do to swing my weight around so I could sit in a chair with that leg elevated.

The level of pain was persisted and so morphine was prescribed. They shot it directly into the IV every four hours. It was a new sensation for me. I could literally feel the medicine move down my body until it reached my feet. It was effective to relieve the pain at that time, but it was so mind-numbing that I could not focus my eyes to read. After a week on that medicine, I progressed to the point it was not needed.

Meanwhile, another major problem was developing. For some unknown reason, I began to retain water. My first indication of it was having difficulty in breathing. My oxygen level fell to just 80, so I was hooked up to oxygen. While it helped to get the oxygen, it did nothing to help me improve my breathing. I don't think it reached the point of pneumonia, but there was significant water in my lungs.

Days passed but I just continued to retain water. The medical staff did not pick up on the issue because I was still very thin and did not look swollen. Even though I complained to the staff, they simply did not understand. A confirmation to me was the daily measurement of my weight. It appeared I was gaining a little weight daily, and they were rejoicing. Eventually, the truth revealed that all the weight was water retention.

I was fortunate that my sister-in-law, Susan, was a local nurse. She became my advocate. On one of her visits, I discussed the situation with her. She immediately went to the nurses' station and explained the situation. They first tried to say that it was simply the result of the medication I was taking. She was able to tell them that I was not on any of those medications that typically had the side effect of weight gain. Finally, the cardiologist was alerted and came for another visit. He wasn't initially convinced that I had a severe problem. The convincing evidence was that my scrotum has swelled to the size of a large grapefruit. Once he saw that, two more medicines were prescribed on the spot.

The medicine was effective and I urinated 40 pounds of water in ten days. Going from 180 pounds to 140 in a short period of time was not a "diet" I would recommend to anyone. Once that water was drained, I came off oxygen and only needed to build the lung capacity up again.

Meanwhile, since I had so little time before returning to the hospital for the second surgery, I had not received any therapy for the rotator cuff surgery. I have known many who even after surgery never regained full range of motion. As I lay in bed, and then sitting in my chair, I performed my own therapy many times a day. Whatever I did worked and today I have 100% range of motion and no discomfort with any use of that arm.

I received many visitors during that time including many who had not visited me at the camp. From that standpoint, it was a great time. The BOP only came by twice that month. I had the phone right by my side and people could call anytime and talk for any length of time.

After 26 days of this ordeal, I ventured to start walking again. Bones were creaking and muscles were tight, but I began walking the hall several times a day even though the speed was slow. I made enough progress in those two days to gain a release from the hospital.

Every few days, a chaplain from the chaplain pool would come by to visit for a few minutes. The hospital had a sophisticated system of receiving email greetings and so the chaplain would bring those. I was told that I received the most communications of anyone in the hospital at the time. The chaplains would visit and then pray before they left. I made great friends of several. When they found out, I would finally be released the entire chaplain staff on that day came to my room. I was presented with a little certificate that designated me as "Chaplain to the chaplains." In spite of my struggles, I had been able to encourage and bless them for their service to me and others.

After 28 days in the hospital for this episode, I was taken back to the facility. There were still a few more surprises in store for me.

Back at the Facility

I was picked up by the camp driver on January 9th. Upon entering, I was taken to the administration building. It was there I was informed the Officer Parsons had filed a complaint against me because he had observed a computer in my hospital room. The computer belonged to my brother-in-law who visited me many times in the hospital.

Prison rules do not allow for any computers. Having access to the internet is perceived as an "escape" with all its available punishments. Eventually, I was cleared because the hospital rooms do not have any wi-fi available and so the complaint was invalid.

My temporary punishment which lasted six weeks, was to be placed in the transfer facility where inmates were locked down 23 hours a day. Since I had only been walking two days, I was still very weak. Being in this other facility put me close to the infirmary and the doctor.

I was able to obtain favor with the evening officer and as such I was able to get out extra time to go walking. The general procedure was that men would line up to pick up their meals and then go back to their cell to eat. Since I was not very mobile yet, my meals were all delivered directly to me.

Linda was in full tax season mode so she was not able to visit very much during that time. Visiting was much more difficult, going thru several screenings into that facility. My brother-in-law, Tim, came fairly often, partly so he could communicate for me with Linda.

On the first Sunday afternoon I was there, I went into insulin shock. My sugar level was just 51. When I first felt it coming on, my roommate gave me some crackers or it may have lower yet. The infirmary was closed and they quickly gave me a couple cans of Ensure. It took a couple hours for the blood sugar to normalize.

When I left the hospital, I had 15 prescribed medicines. The BOP is notorious for not keeping one supplied with proper medicine. I was still taking insulin twice a day and the BOP rarely runs on a consistent schedule. Maintaining a proper sugar balance was a huge challenge. Since the meals were portioned out, I would get about 1800 calories a day—not enough to gain any weight. At the bottom of the weight cycle in the hospital, I had lost to just 135 pounds. By the time I left I was up to 142 and it stayed right there until I came home two months later.

The committee who would decide my "fate" regarding the computer kept putting off meeting with me. Mr. Masters was extremely vengeful and he wanted them to "throw the book" at me. His recommendation, if found guilty, would be the loss of all privileges—no phone, no visits, and no commissary. He also asked for a loss of 14 days "good time" and a maximum of 30 days halfway house/home confinement. The final decision would be made by a Disciplinary Hearing Officer.

There were several bits of irony regarding the use of the computer. One was I was in great pain and they were shooting morphine in my veins every four hours. Needless to say, my eyes would barely focus and my brain was in dumb-down during that time. I could not see the TV screen in the room clearly.

Those were some dark days for me because of the lack of outside contact, especially with Linda. I tried to relay messages via friends there to their families and on, but it was not very successful.

During these days of waiting, I received Judge Walker's decision denying my 2255 motion. It is extremely rare that a judge will overrule his prior decision regardless of how wrong it was. But that would set the stage for another appeal.

It took me a full week to get my phone privileges reactivated. I called Linda immediately but I forgot to transfer additional funds to the phone account so we were cut off after just three minutes. I was issued a cane that same day to assist me in my walking. Standing was especially brutal without the cane. I guessed my leg healing would take another 4-6 weeks, but that proved a bit optimistic. The staph infection had been so severe that my leg from the knee past the ankle was a deep crimson red full of cellulitis. (Seven years after the fact, it is still discolored.) Healing would be accelerated with increased circulation—I could administer some massage, but walking was also a big help.

On March 19, I had my first conference with the Disciplinary Officer and it was refreshing to know he was taking a very lenient approach.

He requested statements from both Tim and Linda and would give a lot of weight against a "very minor infraction."

The very limited food helped to keep my blood sugar down in the 110-120 range. For example, the breakfast was plain oatmeal (no butter, cinnamon, etc.) and a corn muffin. Getting my medicine was also sporadic (except the insulin was delivered twice a day.) All the antibiotics administered during the hospital stay had devastated my digestive system and my appetite. I ate because I needed to and not because it was delicious.

Linda finally made it for a visit the weekend of March 20-21. It was fabulous for many reasons. One was that I was able to be out of the cell for over six hours! When visiting was over, I discovered they had saved me the brunch (sausage, eggs, potatoes and wheat bread.) Because they took their time processing us back in, it took till 3:45p to get back to my room. Supper was served at 4:30p and I was hungry still so I ate that also. It was an indication that my appetite was returning.

Officer Cole who was on duty for the evening shift came to my room and let me out for an hour to walk. He was also kind enough to let me heat a cup of water for a cup of coffee. I had no idea what had prompted the kindness, but I let him know how grateful I was. He continued to allow me that privilege nightly. One night I was out from 6:30p to 9p. Unless one has been confined, it's impossible to know what little bits of freedom mean.

The late evenings also allowed me to start walking up stairs. It was slow going at first. I was able to work up to over 400 stairs per night. That did wonders to my lung capacity as well as improving the strength of my heart.

I also had regularly pain with my rib cage, the after effects of the open- heart surgery. Because I am so thin, the wires that hold my chest together are still prominent with neither muscle nor fat to cover them. I have always been a hard sneezer, and that was devastating to me. It caused a lot of extra chest pain.

April 7th was an interesting day. Computers were being installed for use by the inmates. It would be limited to email, but that would

On Special Assignment

be an incredible advancement and would allow communication to families.

Because the times they would bring insulin were irregular as was the eating times, I was frequently having difficulty with low blood sugar. I have no symptoms with high sugar, but let the count go below 70 and I would begin to react. I kept dried fruit handy so that whenever I would begin to feel faint, eating would bring my sugar back up to normal.

During all this time, my daughter, Roxanne, was making calls to the warden's office. She was very persistent and managed to wade through several layers of bureaucracy to put the pressure on.

It wasn't until April 12 that I learned I qualified for a "diabetic snack" which consisted of two slices of wheat bread and slices of cheese. I quickly accepted that. After eating everything offered me both directly and indirectly, I was able to gain 2 pounds in four weeks. I had had so much tape put on me in the hospital, that after four weeks I was still discovering bits of tape. The skin on my leg no longer looked "angry" as it was going through a second cycle of peeling.

With having so much time "locked down" I was reading about 400 pages a day with whatever was available to read. The time there I read more novels than all the rest of my life put together.

Finally, on Friday, April 16, I was able to meet with the Disciplinary Officers and was told my case was dismissed without reservation. I cannot describe the relief and even elation that I felt. I thanked him profusely. I had a feeling that my friend on the inside had something to do with it although that was never confirmed. But I'm also sure that prayers helped with a divine intervention.

The officer who called me to that meeting asked me afterwards what had been the verdict. He rejoiced with me and allowed me to roam freely the entire morning. Some of the officers at times seemed close to human!

Even though I was cleared, it took an extra five days to get transferred back to the camp next door. I spoke with the administrator, Mr. Johnson, and he promised that if the transfer was not made the next day, he would personally pursue it. That evening I was moved to another room in the facility so that all the men transferring back to camp would be together.

Wednesday evening, April 21, a guard came about 8p to get three of us and move us to the camp. Needless to say, I was mobbed at the camp. Same insisted on carrying my bag of "stuff" back to my cube—the same one I had shared with James. I called Linda and began the conversation with, "I'm back at the camp." That first night back at the camp I hardly slept at all—I guess it was the excitement and relief.

April 28 was a "red letter day." I received my leaving date as May 10. That would make a total of 1029 days of government confinement. I would discover that day that my leg had finally lost its fever—it was cool to touch. That was clear evidence that it was healing.

The next two weeks were simply focused on leaving. There were many goodbyes to say. There were last minutes encouragements particularly to my "preacher boys." Eating all my commissary items, giving things away that I did not want to transport home. Making the final arrangements to travel were a delight.

The day came and I was processed out on Monday, May 10. My personal belongings were all packed and placed in our van. Then we headed out. We met at a Cracker Barrel so we could eat some real food. Friends and family joined us there and what a time of rejoicing it was.

The seven-hour trip to Tampa was uneventful. We checked into the halfway house in Tampa which is run by the Goodwill organization. I arrived timely by 5pm. I was assigned a bed and given food. The typical scenario is for a person to try to find "work" but I was not yet in any kind of physical shape to even look.

I went through the normal interview by the assigned counselor but there was not much he could do to help. He asked Linda to bring me more clothes and other items. One her way to see me on Wednesday, the counselor called her and asked how quickly she could have the house ready because I had been approved to go home. Thursday morning Linda picked me up and I was placed on "home confinement" until my outdate of August 3.

Home confinement usually means one is wearing an ankle bracelet which is hooked electronically to the monitoring station at the halfway house. While one is allowed to go to the store or church, a call must be made before you leave and immediately after you arrive back. For some reason, they could not get the equipment to work properly, and they never bothered to fix it. For almost three months we had this worthless setup. The counselor was not worried about it since he considered me trustworthy.

At the end of the home confinement, I was assigned to a probation officer. She was a nice Christian lady and we had good rapport except for one small incident. I requested travel permission and was always granted it, so other than having to report monthly, it was just a small nuisance. Travel was mostly doing taxes and visiting family.

I made application to renew my Enrolled Agent status with the Internal Revenue Service and it was granted without any reservation or restriction. I even received a call from an IRS attorney in Washington DC to assure me that I was completely validated. Such an irony because the credentials are only given to those whose records are clear. There were no complaints or stains on my record!

It is still a wonderment to me why God allowed all this to happen. As I have studied scripture, it is clear that God often allowed saints to go through many persecutions and trials, almost always unjustly. One only needs to read through Hebrews 11 to see the extent of that. I address a lot of that in my devotional book, Refined Through Suffering.

The Johnny Story

Our paths are not always smooth. One man who lived two cubes down from mine was Johnny. Johnny was from the Chattanooga area and was serving a lengthy sentence for a crack cocaine violation. He was a user, but was convicted as a dealer.

Johnny was African American and was a Muslim. He fiercely hated whites and Christians. Since I was white and Christian, I was an object of his hatred. He did not take any overt action to display his hatred. Rather, he just ignored people he didn't like.

There is a command in the Sermon on the Mount that instructs us to "greet those who don't greet you." See Matthew 5:47. In obedience to the scripture, I began to greet Johnny as I passed by his cube going outside. He simply did not respond. I saw him at other venues as well so I averaged greeting him about five times a day.

I lost actual count but this went on for about eighteen months. That is somewhere in excess of 2500 greetings with no response. The scripture did not say greet and then stop if you don't get a positive response. It simply says, "Greet."

One day as I was walking toward the dorm, I encountered Johnny who was obviously in a hurry. When he saw me, he asked if I was headed for the dorm. This was the first time he acknowledged my existence. I responded that I was and he asked if I could lay a small package on his bed. I was glad to do so.

This was a major turning point in our relationship. He began acknowledging my greetings and would say "Hi." One of Johnny's jobs was the picture taker in the visiting room. On special occasions when Linda was there, we would have our picture taken. Johnny would take the picture on the weekend. During the week, the pictures would be developed and then the two prints (for $1) would be delivered to our dorm room.

On our anniversary weekend, Johnny took our pictures. A week later he came by the cube to deliver the pictures, but there was only one. When I asked about the second picture, he simply said, "You will get it later." I did not question him further at the time. About three weeks later, he came to my cube and presented me with a beautiful hand painted card with the extra picture attached, wishing Linda and me a Happy Anniversary. I was very impressed with his work. I asked him if he would keep the card until Linda came for the weekend.

I requested that he come over during the morning that Linda would be there and make the presentation of the card to her, and let her respond to his generous act of kindness. (He usually charged others about $10 to make his cards.) He did come to our table and presented it to her. She responded by giving him a big hug—it may have been the first white woman he had allowed to hug him. But it was a testimony of God's grace and the effect when we carefully follow the commands of Christ!

Individual Stories

Sherman Williams

One of the first big names that I met was Sherman Williams. He introduced himself to me. Sherman played for the Dallas Cowboys and they won two Super Bowls when he was on the team. His success lured him into illegal drugs and that was the cause of his coming to prison. But that humbling situation caused him to listen to God, and he was living a Christian life. His focus was not complaining or pitying himself for being there. Instead, he was focusing on his future. He desired to help children and youth when he was freed so they can avoid the personal crash that he experienced.

I didn't get to minister to Sherman very long because he was transferred to another facility. He was released in 2014 and seems to be holding true to his redemptive story.

Chico Tillman

It was August 15, 2007 that Chico asked to talk with me. He lived just a couple of cubicles away from me. He told me he wasn't real sure of me when I first arrived. But after watching me for four weeks, he decided that I was "for real."

Chico had already served 13 of his 15-year sentence. In year 6, he had found Christ. A couple years previously to our meeting he felt called to preach. His first eight years were spent in medium-high security, so he was locked down 23 hours a day. It is hard for me to comprehend surviving, but he had. He was only 23 years old when he came to prison—leaving behind a wife and small children.

He spoke in Chapel on a Sunday evening, and he wanted my assessment of his sermon. It was quite good, and I told him so. I was able to offer him suggestions that he realized would make him more effective. He thanked me for the "constructive" criticism. Prior to that I was unaware that he despised palaver intensely.

That led to a conversation on how he could prepare himself for ministry once he was out of confinement. We were able to outline a number of skills that I could mentor him during his remaining time. His parting words that day were, "I believe God sent you here because I've found no one else in 13 years who could help me in this way."

On Special Assignment

The next day Chico came by and dropped off a book he had written, "A Portion of My Soul" for me to read and critique. I have heard recently that Chico is evangelizing all over the world.

Chico would periodically stop by to ask for prayer. Once it was for his mom who was sick. Our prayer groups were gaining a reputation for getting prayers answered.

Chico finally got a transfer date of December 29—but they did not tell him where.

Dr Mike Woodward

One of the first men that I met was Dr. Mike, known to us there as simply "Doc." His story will be a little lengthy simply because it was, but also because my interaction with him was a lot. Born into a modest home in Northern Georgia his early life was simple. But he had great ambitions. From high school he went on to the University of Georgia in Athens. After completing his bachelor's degree, he stayed there to attend law school. Upon completing his law degree, he realized he did not want to practice law, and went on to Mercer University to become a medical doctor. After completing his residency, he moved to Florida and established his own medical practice as well as developed other medical clinics as well. He met his wife there in Macon, and over the next several years had three children, a boy and two girls.

Things went well until he became a "target" of the federal government. His clinic in South Carolina was accused of overprescribing pain medication. It should be noted that he personally never wrote a single prescription there. All the prescription written conformed to the FDA's protocols. Out of some 10,000 patients, the prosecutor claimed that 12 had been harmed.

I personally read hundreds of pages of transcript from the legal proceedings and the case simply had no proof. Another of the unjust judges was bound and determined to make an example. What he accomplished was the destroying of a family, the loss of millions of dollars in tax money, and the further eroding of trust in a government gone amok.

At the conclusion of the process, Doc was sentenced to 15 years. He received the "diesel therapy" treatment. Diesel therapy is being transported between various facilities. Sometimes he was in county jails, sometimes in federal transfer facilities, and other times in various levels of security prisons. In his case, he was literally on the road for some four months. Travel as a prisoner is brutal. The men are handcuffed and shackled. They are often in buses or planes for long periods of time—several hours. They are given sack lunches which they try to eat while handcuffed. Equally challenging would be trying to use the restroom while shackled!

On September 19, 2007, Doc received word that his son was put back into the hospital in St Petersburg FL at All Children's Hospital. He has cystic fibrosis, a birth defect, and has been struggling all of his 15 years. Doc, of course, felt so helpless. I was able to get a message through to Don Keeling, my former executive pastor and he went to visit the son there in the hospital.

But the same day, Doc received word that the Appeals Court had dismissed his appeal on jurisdictional grounds (not on its merit). His attorney was so upset that she filed for an "en banc" hearing (a re-hearing by all eleven judges) and paid the $2500 fee herself. Sometimes the emotional roller coaster was exaggerated, but it certainly was exhausting. Without Christ and His extra grace, I don't know how others survive.

By the time Doc and I had been friends for a month, he expressed a major desire to learn more about scripture and spiritual matters. So we began to meet every day for about an hour. It was apparent from the start that he had an insatiable desire to learn. So in our first meeting, I outlined a full course of study for him.

A short time later, my friend, Dr. Mike received bad news. Back in January he was given a re-sentencing hearing. Because of his cooperation with the government, the prosecutor recommended that his sentence be reduced to time served. But the judge, wielding his unchecked power, only reduced the sentence by two years, meaning he still had many years left on the thirteen years. It was understandable that his spirit was crushed. It was appealed but eventually the appeal was denied. Beyond comfort and a suggestion to trust God for his divine purpose, there was little I could do. But God often takes our disappointments and turns them to His ultimate purpose. God used it mightily his Glory.

On Special Assignment

A few days later Dr. Mike made a personal statement in our Bible study. He had a net worth of about $20 Million prior to his arrest. He lost it all. But in losing all that, he found Christ, and so it was worth it.

It seemed that emotions were always on the move. At times there was overwhelming hope and at other times we were fighting despair. For example, in my September 24, 2007 entry, I wrote, "There seems to be a sense around here that my stay would not be long. So guys were wanting to get as much teaching from me as possible. It's probable that many of those I'm closely associated with would also leave within the next six months." That gave a sense of urgency to all our discipleship efforts.

Early on Doc wanted to become my mentoree. Given his journey up till then, I suggested we concentrate on developing biblical character. He was a vociferous note taker. He knew my stated goal was to make him a "man of integrity." That is not quick work. When he would say something contrary to what we had been learning, he would catch himself and make a correction. But week by week I would him growing in knowledge and grace, and that is the path of discipleship.

My challenge was that I had to prepare all the lessons. While I had been able to get some resources sent in, most of it I had to pull from my memory and my heart. God was faithful, and Mike absorbed a lot of information. As is usual, it takes more time to incorporate it into one's life, but that is the business of discipleship.

Doc seems to soak up everything that I was teaching him, and then tried to put it into practice immediately. He shared that his mom was not able to come down the last couple weeks and it would be at least another week before she could. I always enjoyed meeting and talking with her when she did come, and it was obvious she adored her son.

Doc was persistent in pursuing any legal possibility to get justice. He was constantly working on an appeal—sometimes direct and sometimes the indirect route. Other attorneys in the camp would read his work and research and encourage him along the way. But time and time again, the courts either denied him or ignored him. I don't know which was worse.

In January 2008 I noted that "many times in our sessions we would just talk." He had so many deep hurts in life, that he needed a long time for healing. Even then he expressed his commitment to the process, and he also stated he would be committed to me "for life." He said he would devote his life to supporting whatever ministries God led me in. He wanted to be ordained before I left and we began planning that way, based on his finishing the course of study.

We had a full lesson on "the call of God." I asked him to write out his testimony. After the lesson, he shared his heart. He told me that my coming to Atlanta had been the real catalyst to turn his heart completely to God. God's grace always has a transforming influence.

Early in February Doc's roommate went home. Many of us gathered to see him and four others off that day. When I met with Doc for our daily session, he was feeling the loss intently. Over the years he's been incarcerated, he's seen many people leave and promise to stay in touch—and not one ever has. I told him that in my short time, I had already heard from two different men.

March 1 was a memorable day—it was time for Doc's ordination. We had nine to attend and that made a very full cubicle. It was really exciting to have Steve participate by reading the passage from First Timothy. Ben and Larry were the other readers. We used the ordination service from the Free Methodist Book of Discipline. He answered the questions appropriately. As Doc knelt and had hands laid on him, we could feel the power of the Holy Spirit. He was given the charge to "preach the Word" and challenged to be all God would have him be. Then we presented him with his credentials.

On May 4, Doc received word that his mother had suffered a stroke and was taken to Park Ridge Hospital in Chattanooga. Since she had not given her life to Christ, it became a double concern. Special groups prayed for this earnest request. A few days later she was moved to a Rehab Hospital. With Doc's medical knowledge, he knew the risks and waited until he could get a complete report. They were unable to find the cause of the stroke. He predicted that there would be a major reoccurrence within two years.

After a couple weeks in the rehab, his mother was ready to come home, but only if she could get help to stay with her for the

On Special Assignment

transition. It came as a complete surprise that Doc's wife, Jill, offered to bring the children and go for two weeks. Jill and Dorothy had had a "hate" relationship for nearly the entire twenty years Doc had been married. He had no idea what caused the change of heart, but he welcomed it.

In the following months, it was a great challenge for Doc to speak with his mother on the phone. Her personality was changed and Doc reported that he seemed to be talking to a stranger. It was very difficult for him emotionally so we continued to pray for them both.

In July, Doc's family came to visit for their "semi-annual trip." This time was better than the previous times. He used to go into depression for days before they came and for several days after—nursing his self-pity. Doc had progressed spiritually enough that he didn't mope at all. He was informed that his son had seven cavities and the dentist wanted $1100 to fix them. His daughter Eden needed braces and the orthodontist wanted $6000 for treatment. His earnings from the BOP were about $17 a month, so, obviously, he could not help.

The following month, I saw Doc at breakfast and he was down in his spirit. His phone call with his wife ended with "it would have been better for the children if you had died when you got arrested." I don't profess to understand such cruel statements. I assured him of our being true friends forever and I have kept that promise. It must have impacted him because he told me later in the day how meaningful my statements had meant to him.

Since Doc's friends had basically deserted him, he received little to no mail. His family rarely wrote him so we adopted him as one of ours. I began sharing mail, especially the blogs that Linda wrote and then sent me the printed versions. It helped reconnect him to the outside world.

In Nov 2008, Mike came off "medically unassigned" and began work as a clerk outside the fence. That gave him $45 a month in income which was sorely needed. He confided in me that the real reason of the change was that God had convicted him on his integrity. Being a medical doctor, he had all the right things to say to a doctor to be "medically unassigned." But he really was able. It gave me an opportunity for a teaching moment and that lesson was that kingdom leadership begins with character development.

Doc's job allowed him to drive around the compound picking up and delivering. It made a major boost in his mental outlook. My note was "he almost seems like he's free."

Sometimes there are unexplainable items that arise. For unknown reasons, Doc's oldest daughter concocted a story of sexual abuse. Never mind the fact that Doc had already been incarcerated about 6 years. Nevertheless, cops from Sarasota County came up to interview him. Her story was so inconsistent, it ignored well established facts, and had huge holes in her story. Doc was hurt to the core, as any father would be, even though he was exonerated. Again, it was an opportunity to minister grace in the midst of injustice and his spirits were lifted once again.

I talked with Doc about me transferring to the Jessup facility to be closer to home. He said if I transferred he wanted to do so also. Even though it would be more difficult for his mother to come visit, he figured she was not going to last long anyway. Since his regular family had abandoned him, he saw me as "all he's got."

Doc had issues with the IRS. After his arrest, he was unable to care for tax filing, not having access to the information. In typical government fashion, they took the reported information and created an SFR (substitute for return prepared by the IRS). So they had created an assessment for close to one million dollars. By the time it made its way through the system with penalties and interest, the government obtained a judgment for $1.1 million. He presented the issue to me and we went to work. We created a tax return with the best information we had available, and unbelievably we were able to settle the case for $46.50. So even confined, I was able battle the IRS successfully.

Doc transferred to the camp at Maxwell Air Force base in January 2010. He was released to the half-way house in Chattanooga in 2011. He was able to find work and after a few months was involved in a horrible traffic accident when a semi-truck struck him. The damage was extensive and he ended up in medical facilities for several months. He "coded" more than once, and each time God spared his life.

On Special Assignment

The accident left him permanently injured, but he was able to recover sufficiently to become fully functional. I was pleasantly surprised when he moved to Bradenton FL and we were once again connected. He has renewed his commitment to assist me in all future business and ministries into which God will lead us.

Robert Granda

September 28, 2010

Dear Bob:

I've been promising myself that I'm going to write you tomorrow now for about the last two weeks. I'm sorry I've taken so long, but Sam keeps me up to date on how well you're doing.

This month has been full of excitement for Kim and I as we begin to ready ourselves for our "new start" in life. Kim is trying to get us settled into a place to live. After we found a place, signed a lease, half-way moved in and started exhale a little, we now are fearing the new owners of the complex will not allow felons to live there. Since our verbal agreement went out the door with the old owners, now Kim can't believe we might already be on the market for a new location. Money we worked so hard to save for this day is almost scarce as it is, but we'll make it. I just feel so bad for her now that she is working two jobs a week, Monday – Friday. From 4:30 am to 5 pm and weekends Saturday and Sunday, 2p – 10pm. Here I set still helpless. Even though everything isn't going as we planned, she still makes it to visit with a smile.

(I'm sorry if this letter just got hard to read, but they turned off the lights and it's hard to see my handwriting.)

Sam is well; I helped him a few weeks back with his rebuttal and I pray that will go well for him. We had a few after midnight late nights of proof reading and getting everything in order for typing. In the end, it sounded great and I'm not even a lawyer.

They shipped Judge Teel out last week, but we don't know where yet. He really did a good job transitioning over in Bible study after you left. We will all miss him dearly as we did you. I think Gary Atnip will try to head it up from here, but I fear how well he will be able to hold such a big group together. Truth is, nobody can do what you did for us all. Your friendship and mentoring has changed my life. I've been getting your devotionals from Kenny and they are great. You truly are amazing.

I finally got my release date from Mr. Reynolds. If everything stays on track, I'll be walking out on December 15th!! I'm so glad I don't have any more Christmases and New Year's Days here; six was enough. I just have to pray now that my probation officer doesn't notify our new property management of our situation. I thought the only thing they had to do was verify you address, not tell them that a felon is moving in. Wow, we knew we would have to cross obstacles like this sooner or late, but we were hoping for later.

Well, tell Linda we both said hello. We sure miss seeing her smiling face at visit. Ask her to please tell Todd I said hello as well. I'm going to go for now but I promise I'll write you with the lights on next time.

I just want to thank you and Linda both so much for helping Kim and I build the foundation we are starting our new beginning on. We are looking forward to the time we can share each other's' company once again.

Health & Happiness!! Your friend, Robert

Robert's Testimony: From Convicted Felon to Convicted Christian

I once was lost but ....

As I begin my story, I am writing with the end in mind. Not the end of where my life is heading, but the end in which these words will be the last ones about everything that has led me to where I am now. I want to apologize in advance to the people who hear this and never get to meet me first hand. If is for you that God has directed me to share my story. Without all of your prayers and support these words would never have been possible.

This is the final door for me to personally close on my days of drug deals, addiction, and prison. Those days are dead to me now and so is the self-absorbed person that I used to be. It is my hope that this brings a final closure to everyone's unanswered questions to the occurrences that ultimately created story. Even though I am

On Special Assignment

still learning and growing day-to-day right now, I have reached a point in my life that I have to mark an end to that dark part of my life's journey and the events in it. Some parts of the story are very painful to write about. I am not very proud of some of the events that have unfolded in my life up to this point. It is filled with shame and embarrassment to me, my wife, my family, and most importantly my God. This is not an explanation of who I used to be, but an introduction to who I have become.

"Carry each other's burdens, and in this way you will fulfill the law of Christ. If anyone thinks he is something when he is nothing, he deceives himself." Galatians 6:2 – 3

Make no doubt about it, everyone who hits bottom on a journey that is infected with drugs has to start somewhere. The beginning is different for everyone, tragically the bottom is painstakingly the same. Despite the thousands of ways that people get started on that journey, it only takes one careless wrong step to send you spiraling down and for me that step was taken out of a life of normalcy.

My life never had any of the precursor signs that one might think necessary to fall victim to an involvement with drugs. Great parents, a solid education, and successful employment, I was on track and focused on good things to come. I had hopes and dreams just like everyone else. My future looked bright and I was in total control of my life, or so I thought. Truth is no one is ever in total control of their life. There is just no such thing as "total control." Life is filled with problems and unseen obstacles every day which take calculated choices to overcome the pressure of choice was one of my first downfalls. Irresponsible choices that eventually change the direction of my life's "on track" journey. It's where and when in my life that I was faced with those choices that lead me to take my first bail steps toward drug use. I didn't want anyone to see me as someone who couldn't control their own life. He became incredibly harder for me to hide what the toxic cocktail of drugs and money was doing to me and my life. Tormented daily with addiction, the consequences of my choices were beginning to unfold. So this is where my story begins.

I tried to think back to the time where I started losing control of my life, but no specific moment comes to mind. I am pretty sure it is when I stop letting God into my life that things begin to go wrong.

Actually, I had gotten my life before all this happened, but it was the mountain and asking back in again. While! That's not an easy thing to admit. Sent had a tight hold on my life and it was by my own choices I suffered in it. I really don't think that anyone can look back and pinpoint the moment they got off track. Whatever the crack was for me that led my life to crumble was too small for me to notice at the pace that I was living. I could never get somewhere or something fast enough in my life. I could slow down enough to realize that my life had stopped moving forward. I was stuck in a race to nowhere with prison for the price

Sometimes I wonder why it is so easy for people to look back for something or someone to blame. At the same time, why is it so hard to just take responsibility for your own poor decisions and move forward from there I? When I finally did, I realize that I had to keep going and growing. I once read that the error of youth is to believe that intelligence is substitute for experience, while the error of old age is to believe that experience as a substitute for intelligence. The truth is it doesn't matter how old I am, I can't ever stop growing. I have learned to be content with what I have, but not with who I am. My personal growth is like riding a bike, I'm either moving forward or I'm falling off and I'm tired of falling off.

"Brothers, I do not consider myself yet to have taken hold of it. But one thing I do: forgetting what is behind and straining toward what is ahead, I press on toward the goal to win the prize for which God has called me heavenward in Christ Jesus." Philippians 3:13 – 14

Most people who have never been involved with drugs or the lifestyle that comes with it have a hard time understanding how someone they knew so well becomes the victim. Your family never sees it coming, your boss has no idea, your friends have their own problems to focus on, and you yourself never thought it could happen to you. You see, selling drugs gave me an insight, close-up look at a lot of different levels of addiction. Most people were the party-type crowds, while others were the pity- type crowds. The common denominator about all of them is, once you find drugs for whatever reason the first time, they will find you from there on out.

I saw it split up relationships, divide families, and terminate employments. Drugs can make people feel good, or they can make them feel bad. Some people get lost, or others get found. They can

On Special Assignment

make you laugh or they can make you cry. They can make you feel alive or they can help you die. Like I said, I have seen just about every angle there is, and the price people end up paying cost them a lot more than it ever did to get into their hands in the first place.

Looking back on how I could have ever played such a role in facilitating such a profound cycle of self-destruction makes me feel so ashamed. The tales of other people's addiction that I could tell her almost endless. One of the most impossible aspects of it all was that I was never surprised and just who and how many people were ever involved. In just months after I was sucked into the game, I saw police officers, doctors, attorneys, business owners, and even a teacher who was right in the middle of an addiction. The numbers are staggering and chances are you past people every day that you have no idea about the struggles they are hiding. No one is ever safely out of reach. What's more shocking than that was I was the guy they all called to enable their sickness. The more diverse clientele, the more accepted that people made it all seem. I guess from the popularity of everything was where I started to get the help I needed in justifying how wrong in all was.

Slowly but surely it took me over just like it does everyone else. Graham, ounce, pound, dollar after ill-gotten dollar the money poured in and I thought I had everything under control. Lie after lie, it just got easier and easier. Everyone was doing it, but didn't want anyone else to know. It gets to people so bad that once I knew two people who were using drugs while living in the same house together and neither one wanted the other to find out. Sound crazy? Well, that's what it does to you, it makes you just that.

I was lost and living in my own world were making the rules (or the law for that matter) wasn't wrong as long as I got away with it. Every day my own addiction to drugs, money, and lifestyle got worse and worse. I even started pushing away people who were close to me. I stopped trusting everyone. Everything I said was a lie and it felt like the truth when he said. Moments of clarity were sporadic and ignored. I manipulated, I was selfish, I was consumed with immaturity, and I started doing whatever I felt. I was elevating my own needs and wants above the people I was hurting the most. I was unstoppable in my own mind. Everything was by my own decision and hidden at the root of it all was my blind and blatant lack of self-respect.

The haunting images that I have to live with now are painful reminders of just how far down drugs can take and that I took people. I knew of single moms who took it back to the store for drug money, to beauty pageant queens that traded their looks for the next time. I watch people stay awake for weeks at a time with no sleep, to a bank or do a line of cocaine off his desk after hours. The arm of addiction reached everyone empathetically I was the hand attached to it.

I saw it as fast money. Some saw it as supplying the party, while others sought is just selling drugs, but in the race nobody seemed to see it for what it really was except one person. Even after my arrest, all the lawyers, FBI, ATF, and DEA agents, rooms full of police, jail guards and judges, nobody saw it like my mother. It was at a time that I thought there were not any words left that could help or hurt me because I had trained my mind to only listen to myself. She said to me, "you're not a drug dealer, your murderer! You are poisoning our community!" She was right. Suddenly after all of the threats and shakedowns, searches and scare tactics, she was the one who really said it like it was. I was poison. Still, even then I tried to justify things with thoughts like: "I never pushed the stuff on anyone; no kids ever got anything from me; I never took someone's last dollar; if they don't get it from me, it will just be someone else tomorrow." Who was I kidding? My time was up. It was game over. I needed a plan and so I prayed for one. That prayer was nothing more than a whisper to myself. Small and tiny, forgotten at first, but slowly got manifested it into my life. The temptation that drugs offered me began to fade away.

"No temptation has seized you except what is common to man. And God is faithful; he will not let you be tempted, he will also provide a way out so that you can stand under it." 1 Corinthians 10:13

For me, it was never just one bad choice or one bad decision. They just kept coming, one right after another until my entire life was consumed. Everything I did and every lie I told emerge from my own selfish motivations. It wasn't easy keeping up with so many different lives and lies. All my energy and time was a fantasy self in which lack character and integrity. The path of my destruction and addiction was no longer unique to me. I was an overload mode from a lethal combination of ignorance and self-absorption.

All of a sudden my case was no different than anyone else. I was plagued with everything my new lifestyle and brought me, money, drugs, sex, alcohol, freedom, and influence, but I was still empty inside. Too far end to turn back, the unthinkable happened in my house of cards came crashing down. The madness of it all that screamed in my head was finally quiet. It was over and I knew that there were only a few ways that you could ever get out of the drug game and at least I was still alive.

I was caught, arrested, and convicted. The details of my casing crime are all insignificant now. The twisted tales of my indictment painted a picture of a monster fueled by greed and tricked by addiction. I could no longer ignore reality, shame, or embarrassment. My legal realities confronted me and I was sentenced to seven years in federal prison for conspiracy to traffic meta-phentermine and possession of a firearm. I was in a frozen state of the disbelief. For the first time in my life I was forced to face the inevitable consequences of my action. There is a lot of irony in having to take responsibility for being irresponsible.

The simple fact is, I was drawn off the path of life that God has for me and down a road filled with self-destruction and ultimately prison. Prison, the word itself still chokes me up to say it. Rock bottom, seemingly futureless, scared, and disoriented, I entered my sentence not knowing what awaited ahead of me.

Prison, for the most part, is a concrete jungle where dreams come to die. It is where the feeling of being alone can, at times, you will live one bite at a time from the inside out. It is where the beginning of the end starts for so many, but has become a second chance at life for me. I knew that part of getting that second chance was taking responsibility for the mess that I have made in the first place. These are the times in life when we must go on alone and draw from God the strength to do it, knowing that he will never fail us. In the beginning when you are caught people around you say, "well, I certainly hope that you learned your lesson." Well, the real lesson doesn't come until you can learn to open up your heart and mind to God and trust in his plan for you.

I don't think that I could have worked any harder at failing and falling than I did back then. Once I hit bottom, the climb back up seemed hopeless and long. I think for a lot of people it is easier to just sink into a hole of self-pity and drown yourself in an unheard song of remorse. Quietly you might even think to pray for some kind of deliverance, but your faith at the bottom is as empty as all the promises and lies you told to get yourself there. Don't forget, I whispered that little prayer. Lost without any values and any kind of perspective for life, God did hear me and so my faith began.

"For it is by grace you have been saved, through faith, and this is not from yourselves, it is the gift of God." Ephesians 2:8

The loss of material comforts can move us to simplify our lives. It is in that simplicity that these questions arise to think about:

- How many times in life have you heard the words "count your blessings?"
- How many times in life have you ever tried to do that?
- Can you remember what your last blessings was?
- How many of us pray for something that we get blessed with, but forget to give the thanks back to God for it?

These are the questions that should challenge each of us, even when we are at our worst. These are the questions that my story has answered for me in my life. My deliverance wasn't one big blessing that changed my life at one time. It was on small blessing at a time. Each time that God blessed me, my faith in my prayers grew and comforted me from the afflictions that once poisoned me and my thinking. Through those questions God started to reveal to me my healing.

Nevertheless, I will bring health and healing to it; I will heal my people and will let them enjoy abundant peace and security." Jeremiah 33:6

Sometimes I couldn't help but to wonder if God ever lost sight of me. Was I ever so far gone that I was in danger of never being able to make it back out of it all? Although I could never see it, I was living a life that was reckless and filled with constant danger. One that could have easily gotten me killed every day I chose to do it.

On Special Assignment

As I have explained, there wasn't much keeping me grounded in the whirlwind of my drug induced insanity. It is crazy that I can look back on that time now and recognize one of the greatest blessings I have ever received.

There I was trapped in the middle of some of my worst days and the one person in my life who ever tried to keep me grounded through it all was the one person that I kept taking for granted. How could I have ever known that in and through it all I would somehow end up falling in love. What a blessing that she turned out to be in my life, one that I thank God for every day.

Back then I never told her that I loved her even though she would always make a point to tell me, but I'll never forget the day I finally said the words to her. It was late one night a few weeks before I was arrested and I was about to leave the house. She sat in the middle of her bed crying and begged me to stop everything and just stay home with her. I said, "I feel like everything is going bad. Everything is starting to close in on me. I don't want anything to happen to me without you ever knowing how I feel about you. I love you, Kim, and a part of me always has." Then I turned away and walked out the door. I was gone again into the night, which turned into days before I saw her again.

It is hard on me to this day to know that I am probably responsible for some of the hardest tears she ever had to cry. I tried to get her to leave me more than once. I lied to her on numerous occasions without even blinking. I left her home alone for days and nights on end without even a call. I even cheated on her before we were married. She has had to fact and overcome some of my darkest confessions I've ever had to make.

I don't know how someone as sweet and special as her could ever make it through the living hell that I drug her through. It's been said that the highest and ultimate example of love is forgiveness. Well, I have never seen such a power of forgiveness like she has been able to share with me. Her love and continued support has proven to me that she could have only been heaven sent. No matter how bad I looked to the rest of the world, she was the only one who never lost sight of the good in me. Her perseverance to make things work between us was unfathomable. I never know what real love felt like until she came into my life.

We have been married now for almost three years. We were married in prison. How incredible of a woman do you have to be to take a man with no money, no car, no home and no security (and at the time not very much of a future either) into your life forever. I have no words that will ever be able to describe the value and love that I have for my wife. I can only say that she is the blessing of all my blessings and I have vowed to love her for the rest of our days.

"He who finds a wife finds what is good and receives favor from the Lord." Proverbs 18:22

She has stayed and supported me through every minute of every day. She is really the only person who can testify to how far I have come from the beginning. Her positive influence has helped me from the start to begin seeing myself at the end of all of this. She has been the only one who has stood beside me and believed in me no matter what for every inch of every mile.

I wish now that somehow I could have made it out of all my troubles without her. I would give anything to have saved her from all the pain I undoubtedly put her through, but the truth of it all is that she saved me with all her love. In the darkest part of my journey it was her undying love that gave me reason to fight my way back.

"Husbands, love your wives, just as Christ loved the church....." Ephesians 5:25

I do just that.

She is also the reason I have made this promise to never again live, look, or discuss anything about the days of the past again. I owe her my every tomorrow from here on out and we both have agreed that we have endured enough of this for the rest of our lives already. Our time and energy will be spent from now on unfolding the plans that we have spent the last six year dreaming about.

I understand that my story might be an inspiration that someone else might need someday. That is why I am sharing it with everyone now, because it will be up to the souls who carry it forward with them to pass it along. I have said before that a million dollars and a million words could never change my yesterdays, so I have to focus on today and keep planning my tomorrows. So you see, one of the

On Special Assignment

reasons that I wrote this now is, even though this story is mine, it won't be mine to tell anymore once I am home.

Trying to absorb everything that has happened to me took a lot of time to process. All of the negativity, anxiety, and mistakes I made have played over and over in my head a thousand time, each time highlighting all the ignorance and shortcomings in my life. You see the pain wasn't when I hit bottom because I knew that if I stayed in long enough it was bound to happen. It wasn't looking at all the faces that I had lied to and that had lost trust in me. The real painful part came at the turn-around point. There is no way about, change hurts! It hurts because you find yourself in a place that you don't know how to get out of, or even know where to start.

Nevertheless, I was willing. I needed reconstruction and I was motivated to rethink and rebuild every aspect of my life. I am proof that it is never too late for God to remake someone. It might have taken prison for me in my situation, who know. The truth is, everyone has some kind of personal prison in their own life that can, could, or is holding them back from experiencing the life that God has planned for them.

Once I started my walk with God I realized the promises that He has before me are greater than the pain that is behind me. So on November, 19, 2005, I got saved and began my transformation. It took a lot of guidance and strength to break me of my stubborn ways and ignorant thinking. Guidance, which ironically, I received from guys I have met in prison. It was quite some time before I realized this wasn't just God's plan for me to create a principled centered life for myself, it was his best plan. I knew right then that I couldn't give up my tomorrows by building any more monuments of my past failures.

"Consecrate yourselves, for tomorrow the Lord will do wonders among you." Joshua 3:5

From the inside out I began to change. First, my heart and mind, and next the physical "me" changed. (Yeah, I lost 100 pounds!)

Prison is specifically designed to break a person down to nothing. Intimidation tactics are sharp and harsh and after you name is replaced by a number, you really have to start fighting to get yourself back; but how does one accomplish this? This is a question it takes a lot of time to decide on. For me, I had to start by slowing down and reconsidering my life and what I wanted out of it. I really had to take my time to find myself again and, first, I had to be sure that I had learned from all my mistakes. I had to adopt a new perspective on my life. I knew that I had to climb mountains of suffering while holding onto God's promise. I had to rebuild my shattered relationships with my family and friends, but the most important thing was I could never stop growing from that day on. My life was my new lesson to learn from and build on.

Grow and build, that is exactly what I have done ever since I have simplified my life and re-arranged my thinking. I have rebuilt my character and learned to live with integrity. I have discovered an invaluable insight from my time here in prison, one that has changed my life forever. I have learned to invest my time in personal connections with people rather than material consumption. I have enjoyed the richness of spending time with my wife and getting to know her better. I have regained the balance in my life and learned not to be victimized by other peoples' influence. I have stopped spreading myself too thin by pursuing too many things in too many different directions. I have learned to think clearly and make proactive decisions from which to build a firm foundation. I have taken the time to understand the power of forgiveness by seeking it from the people that I have hurt, and offering it to the people that have hurt me. The critical key to my own personal transformation came when I learned to forgive myself. In fact, I believe it is the only way to ever break the shackles of pain with which addiction holds on. Grow, love, forgive, and allow God to direct our steps from now on so that we make the most of the opportunities He provides for us; that's it.

Prison was just one of God's investments for my life. From now on, it is with God and through God that I will accomplish all of my life's dreams and goals. Every journey in life has to come to an end, but it is in the end that you realize it was the journey that matters most. My journey will not always be easy, living with felonies and failures will always present challenges, but rest assured with God on my side and in my heart, I will make it.

On Special Assignment

"I can do everything through him who gives me strength." Philippians 4:13

A very good friend of mine once shared a very valuable lesson in life with me. He said, "Live simply, care deeply, speak kindly, and leave the rest to God." He was one of the wisest men I knew. It's just that simple.

I want to thanks everyone for the love and support that has reached me through all of your prayers. I also want to give a special thanks to my incredible parents for their never ending love, patience, and not ever giving up on me even though I gave them a million reasons to do so. I also want my beautiful wife, Kim, to know that without the power of her love I don't think that I'd even be here today. Thanks to my God for his grace and giving me the strength to keep getting back up for the climb.

I want to dedicate this story to the thousands of souls out there that are still lost. Not everyone makes it back out like I have. So tonight and every night I'll whisper another prayer for them. Amen.

……now I am found.

God Bless!

Robert Granda, Jr.

10/29/2009

(Thanks, Bob, for all of you support and guidance! Knowing you have helped me write this. Your friend, Robert)

Robert was one who took discipleship very seriously. He faithfully attended and participated in the daily afternoon bible study groups He expressed himself as truths of scripture enlightened him, and was very encouraging to the others in the groups.

Jack Nash

Jack came to Atlanta in early part of 2008. He had previously served as a pastor and missionary with the Seventh Day Adventists. His "crime" had to do with tax issues in non-profits. His wife, Jan, came to visit most every weekend since their home was near Apison, TN, a little village just over the Georgia border.

On July 24 we learned that their house had burned the previous night after being struck by lightning. Living as frugally as they did, they didn't have an overwhelming amount of possessions, but the fire took them all. Being incarcerated was particularly frustrating since it severely put a burden on his wife. It seems often that troubles multiply, but God always supplies grace.

Part of the time Jack worked in the laundry room. We worked out a trade—he would do my laundry and deliver my clothes folded neatly to my cubicle. In return, I would give him tax and legal advice. He also had access to get extra apples, and so I would bake them with special cinnamon and butter, and we would split the batch. It was great for both of us!

--Federal Rag Master

Kary Head

Kary became a good friend during our time together. He was born and reared in Morgan City LA (Evangeline Country). He lived a while in Alexandria, not far from where I spent part of my childhood. His "crime" was selling items over the internet where his suppliers failed to deliver on the merchandise.

Kary had his time away from God, but these trials caused him to seek the Lord again. He and Lisa were married just before he came to Atlanta. He was deeply involved in our bible studies, attended classes in our bible school, and was an outstanding bass singer in our Southern Gospel quartet.

Kary and Lisa established their own car sales lot, and we have been privileged to visit them in their home in Northern Georgia.

Dr Ben Marston

Ben was a podiatrist who had crossed the government regarding tax issues. Ben had an interesting journey as it regarding churches. His faith had survived poor treatment at many different kinds of churches. It was hard to find a specific adjective to describe him, so we settled on "eccentric." Nevertheless, Ben wanted to develop a prayer ministry. I mentioned earlier that we established a thirty minute a day time where would try to pray over all the requests that we had received.

Ben had studied church history to a great extent and so we appointed him to prepare some lessons. He wrote five 45 minute sections. We did have to limit him to those 45 minute sections or he would have easily given us twice that much.

After leaving Atlanta, Ben and his wife moved back to Arkansas where he again regained his license as a podiatrist.

Dr Fabian Aurinac

Fabian came from South Texas where he practiced as a cardiologist. He was an avid learner, and desired to follow God. After leaving confinement, he currently lives in Puerto Rico, where we stay in contact.

Todd Griffin

Todd was reared in a Christian home and was an enthusiastic Christian. He was involved in real estate and was a victim of the market crash in 2008. It was one of those unnecessary prosecution where there had been no intentional fraud.

Todd displayed his devotion to Christ in many ways. We became friends with his parents, and his sister. Unfortunately, his first marriage did not survive the imprisonment. Upon his release, he was able to find a new career. He remarried and became stepfather to two, and then added a handsome little boy.

Lee Robbins

Lee was a pastor from the local area. Born and reared in Texas, he had given his heart to God as a teenager, and then responded to a call to preach. After college, he chose to go to Oral Roberts University where he earned a Master of Divinity Degree. He had established a tax service there in Oklahoma. When they decided to move to the Atlanta area to plant a church, he hired a man to continue the business there. The fellow he hired engaged in unethical practices but the prosecutor charged Lee since he owned the business. Not having the funds nor good legal help to defend himself, he ended with a prison sentence.

The trial circumstances were deplorable. In the middle of his trial, the court appointed attorney caved in to the government and in his closing arguments stated the government had won the case and Lee was guilty. Lee discovered during the last of the trial that his attorney had not filed or paid taxes for the previous five years and was at risk for prosecution himself if he didn't let the government win. I learned of much similar corruption as I examined many court documents.

Lee was obviously "shell-shocked" and struggled to understand it all. God allowed me to help him put things into perspective and he gained much spiritual ground. Even though a proper appeal was filed describing the deplorable actions of the attorney, the courts simply ignored it.

After entering the camp in Atlanta, Lee quickly engaged in leadership in the chapel services. When I arrived on the scene, it was natural for us to work together. There were always issues in directing the chapel just like there is on the "outside." Styles of music were a challenge. Since 70% of the population there was black, it was natural for them to dominate the style. But preaching styles were just as much an issue as were music styles.

I worked with Lee on getting all those in leadership to meet and agree. He told me that he had learned more practical information on pastoring the first three months, than in his three years of seminary. Dealing with various personalities with a minimum of conflict is something no seminary seems to be teaching. Lee followed my suggestions and found that an explosive situation was defused.

As is usual in the black culture, titles are important. So Lee designated himself and me as "apostles." I had developed great relationship with the blacks there and so they accepted me as one of their spiritual leaders. While Lee took most of the administrative functions, he made it known to the others that I was his mentor and that he would confer with me on all decisions.

On Special Assignment

After working with Lee for several months, we reviewed some of the basic material on salvation. Jesus' instruction is for men to "repent." While we had concluded that the government's charge against him was totally false, he reached a conclusion that he was not "guiltless." He wrote out his own 51st Psalm and read it to me. He specifically addressed his issue of pride and now believed that God sent him to prison to break his pride. Ironically, several of us had observed others resisting his leadership because of pride. He wanted God to rework his heart so that he could teach the material with his life, that others would clearly see God coming through rather than himself.

Lee was invited to speak to the Nation of Islam group at the camp. (Color stopped me from being invited.) He took the opportunity to share with them a gospel message. Surprisingly, he was invited to return.

July 13, 2008 was the day Lee preached his farewell message in chapel. We moved that evening service up to 5 pm so we could have time for a time of fellowship. The turnout was good—even a few Moslems came to the service and stayed for the fellowship. To close the service, we had Lee kneel and many gathered around him as I prayed a special blessing on him for his future ministry. Pizza, chips and cookies made up the food offering.

The next morning, we walked him to the front shortly after 8a and R&D was already calling him. I said our goodbyes and did not wait to see what time Kim would actually pick him up. They were generous in giving him two hours to report to the half-way house.

Lee and his wife, Kim, have planted a church in the Northeast Atlanta area. We have been privileged to worship with them there. Lee is also employed by the State of Georgia in a program that helps ex-convicts to meld back into society.

Karsten Brinson

I have mentioned Karsten much in my writings above. He was a very shy fellow when I first arrived but he became very passionate about serving the Lord. He expressed a sense of a call to ministry, and I felt that God was indeed calling him. His commitment to a consistent Christian life and to the study of scripture validated that calling.

In addition to his attending the bible college classes, I personally mentored him on average of 5-6 hours a week. His growth in spiritual character as well as ministry skills was remarkable. Upon his completion of the course of study, I ordained him. The service was sealed with the Holy Spirit's presence.

The following week as I preached my "farewell" message, Karsten was designated as the heir apparent of the chapel ministry. The acceptance by the whole congregation was powerful.

On Christmas Day, 2012 I received the following email from Karsten. "Have a great day. I still have yet to meet a preacher that has come through here and walk you walk....thanks for being such a great example of a real man."

Since he was from the Atlanta area, he was able to make quick connections with ministries, and is currently serving as a staff position with a local church there in Atlanta.

Terry Woodard

Terry was another of the men to join bible school. He was an ardent student, and one of those whose temperament was described as "steady." He, too, developed well during my time there.

Upon release, he planted a church on the southside of Atlanta.

Gary Atnip

Gary was a CPA who was falsely accused in an investment scheme. For that he received a ten-year sentence. He was a faithful follower of Christ, and was a great friend during the time in Atlanta.

After release, he returned to the Nashville TN area. We remain in contact.

Kenny Kessinger

Kenny was a delightful Tennessean who got off track in his life and got involved in the drug world. He acknowledged his crime and accepted his punishment. In prison, he returned to following Christ.

He was transferred to the Pensacola FL camp to go through the drug rehab program. His wife moved to Clermont FL while he was in Atlanta. Upon release, he went to that home. They have two daughters who have now blessed them with several grandchildren.

Larry Roundtree

Larry was a retired Baptist preacher from Georgia. As I previously mentioned, he was one of the first men to greet me when I came into the camp. Larry was just a little older than I, but he had multiple medical problems. Getting medical treatment in the BOP was a joke.

Larry had a problem with his bowels and desperately needed a colonoscopy and the Physician's Assistant who led the medical office at the camp agreed. But month after month, it was postponed. Larry appealed to the Warden's office and could not get any action. So he appealed to the Regional Office in order to get results. In the meantime, he had been so persistent with the counselor that he finally wrote a reprimand and placed it into his file.

Once the colonoscopy is completed and it confirms the medical issues, that reprimand should be removed. Other times he suffered from kidney stones, but medical help was non-existent. So he was left to suffer.

Larry's eyesight was deteriorating so he requested a new bible. Our friends, the Stimacks, were gracious in sending him a nice large print study Bible. He was so excited and grateful when it arrived.

Larry is now back in GA, and Doc and I were privileged to visit him in his home.

Alfredo Rivera

Testimony from Alfredo Rivera ...

First, I give all honor and glory to our Lord and Savior Jesus Christ; for having a divine appointment set for me with such a spirit filled, holy and ready to give of all that God has given him, type of man like Robert Bedford. For three years straight of my imprisonment, I have spent no less than four hours a day in the Word of God. The

Word has given me new dreams and inspirations of what He wants me to do when I leave prison. But the privilege to spend at least one hour a day with a man of God who has lived and walked most of what I aspire or/and dream of, can only be a divine appointment. Amen! Robert's clear understanding and ability to share in the Word and bring it to life can only come from the Holy Spirit himself. A man, as myself, who lived for the world for thirty-seven years, then suddenly get called by Jesus Christ, is an eye opening experience to say the least. And, yes, the Holy Spirit is our ultimate teacher, but to learn or to be confirmed what we have come to believe from the Holy scriptures, by a seasoned man of God like Robert, is like the missing piece to a puzzle being put into my spirit to strengthen me in my walk. His teaching and confirmation of the Word in my life is the Lord sending forth a master builder who has built much in the Kingdom and has come to prepare me "solidly" for the journey that awaits me. Robert's way of subtle teaching not only has taught me of the Word but how is best to go about sharing it without condemning the person I am sharing with.

I have never met personally a man who has devoted his whole life to God since he was seven years old. But it sure does feel good in my spirit to know when I am talking with him, that I am sharing with many, many years of godly experience in a not so godly world. I feel it is a true blessing that Robert has opened his life and taken an interest in teaching me all that he does! I pray that I can have a life long relationship with him that will grow more and more every day. And that the Lord helps me hear his calling in my life with Robert. I can only end with saying, I don't know yet 'why me', but I love Jesus for choosing me to meet and learn under one of his preferred and chosen saints! Amen!!

Sincerely,

Alfredo P. Rivera

On Special Assignment

Samuel Gray

One of the great delights was meeting Sam Gray. By profession, he was a CPA. What landed him in prison was that he owned a party boat that operated off the Atlantic Coast. He had several investors, one of whom was a banker. Unbeknown to Sam, the banker (president of his own banking company) was embezzling money from his bank to invest. The feds caught up with him, and he was sent to prison. But the feds also charged Sam with receiving stolen funds and sent him to prison for ten years, as well as his wife for three years.

I read the transcripts of the trial and am thoroughly convinced that he was innocent. He didn't know the true sources of the funds nor did he conspire to receive the investment dollars.

In spite of the injustice, Sam had a great attitude and was honorable in all his actions. Two daughters and a son came to visit him, as did his brother-in-law. Because his wife was also incarcerated for some time, it was about three years before she was able to come. They were able to write, but they had last talked in May 2008 and then it was December 2009 before they were able to talk again. The opportunity to talk came when she was being transferred from a Florida facility to one in West Virginia. Her daughter provided the transportation and he could call her cell phone. He was able to talk with her three times that day, and he was on Cloud 9. When she was freed and able to come visit, what a reunion that was!

Sam had previously been introduced to Christianity by Martin Rosenthal, who had converted from Judaism to Christianity about 30 years earlier. Sam was like a lot of others I have met who exclaimed, "I don't reject Jesus as the Messiah." Sam was a process thinker, and he was still trying to get things settled in his own mind.

Discussions continued on the subjects of integrity and forgiveness. The Jewish law of "eye for an eye" and "love you friends and hate your enemies" contradict Jesus's words "love your enemies." He didn't reject Christ's words as not being virtuous, but was struggling to get there emotionally. Often our discussions would take place as we walked a mile or two on the track.

Sam began attending chapel whenever I would speak. One evening I spoke from Ezra 7:10. He shared with Doc afterward that he was in awe and he had leaned an immense amount of new information.

Sam continued to read several devotionals a day and started attending the afternoon Bible study daily. He told me he had started ending his prayers, "In Jesus' name." After supper, we would often walk and talk. He continually asked questions and showed no resistance to the truth. He continued to struggle with "loving your enemies."

Sam shared a personal story. When he was born, his name was Samuel Abraham Greensburg. When he was about eight, his family moved to Miami Beach where his dad practiced medicine. Even though it was virtually a complete Jewish community at the time, his father decided to change the family name to Gray, and changed his middle name to Andrew. He never asked why; he just accepted it at the time.

As Passover time came around, Sam wanted to talk more about the Jewish traditions. The BOP was accommodating and provided special meals. Since it was a lot of fish, and some of that community did not like it, I was more than happy to trade food. The BOP also accommodated time and space to experience a Seder. I explained the biblical significance of its many aspects, and Sam found that fascinating.

Sam felt included in my family so whenever I received pictures from Linda, I always shared them with Sam. He would be so excited he would kiss the pictures. Sam would also share his pictures. His wife, Marilyn, sent him a little poster where she had interposed pictures of them on a motorcycle. She added captions and we both thought it was cute.

Sam was a reluctant participant in walking. He knew it was good for him, and so he would walk with me but not without some good-natured complaining. So at least once a day, I would coax him into walking with me and it was usually at least 1.5 miles. Being his consistent reminder to get his exercise earned me the name of "Heartless." Years later (I've been gone over six years as of this writing) that name has stuck in Sam's memory and so it headlines every letter received from him!

On Special Assignment

I nicknamed him LES (Lame Excuse Sam) because of his constant resistance to walking and giving me lame excuses. I eventually wrote his wife, Marilyn, to give her a complete report. It brought a huge howl of laughter from Sam when he read it!

Sam dearly loved his wife, Marilyn, and his mood was up or down depending on how long it was since he had a letter from her. She was delighted with the "report" I sent her on Sam, and said she would frame it when she got home.

It was my privilege to order Sam a study bible. I did not tell him when I did. One day he received it with his name engraved, and like all the others, he was excited. Mike finally told him the origin of the gift and he came running out on the track to find me. He declared it was the most meaningful gift (outside of family) he had ever received. He hugged me several times—a kid at Christmas would not have been more excited. He even showed it to the visiting rabbi that next day.

For the first time in his life, Sam had become a daily bible reader. That, to me, was a great success. It was also fun just to teach him what a concordance was and how to use it. He had not previously had any experience with "cross references" and how to connect various bible verses. Sam and I had many different connections, but it was a friendship that would last long beyond the Atlanta time.

As is often the case, the IRS jumps in for anyone convicted of a crime, and tries to make a case for additional taxes. Sam received a Notice of Deficiency for $145,669 plus penalties and interest. The total bill would have exceeded $200,000. He brought the Notice to me and I prepared a proper tax return, as well as the Tax Court Petition. I was filed and working through the process by mail, we were able to obtain a Tax Court decision of a ZERO balance. It was just one of the many victories won during the incarceration.

On January 5, 2010, Sam was awakened by officers at 12:30a and they told him to "pack out." That meant he was leaving. The Officer did not know why or where he was going. He left early the next day with no idea of his "landing place." It took us several days to find out that he had been summoned to testify in another trial and was simply being transferred to a local facility near the court where the trial was occurring. Those days while Sam was gone meant some changes in the daily schedule.

Sam would tell me before I left for home that he was grateful for coming to prison because God allowed me to enrich his life more than he could imagine. He considered that worth more than his freedom.

Sam is now out and we continue to stay in contact. He is currently living in South Carolina with his son. Hopefully, in the near future we will able to see each other face to face.

Dr Greg Clarke

On February 15, 2008 a new man arrived from Birmingham AL. He was a black pastor of a large church there. As I understand it, he testified on behalf of the governor during his trial. As a result, the government pursued him and found a minor tax matter for which he was unaware. His arrival was accompanied by a busload of parishioners and about fifteen carloads of people from his church. Even TV helicopters were filming his arrival—obviously, a man of considerable influence.

When he first arrived, he had decided that he would use this time as a retreat. He would confine himself to his cube and do some significant reflection as well as planning. I was moved to visit with him and talk about the great need for him to interact with the men. Since around 70% of the population here was African American, there was ample opportunity for him to share his heart and message with men who desperately needed his spiritual direction. While I had excellent relations with the black population, his communication skills with that culture were far superior. After praying about it, he came to realize that while his circumstances were undesirable (being in prison), he could be mightily used to God to develop men in the Kingdom. He joined the ministry team, and fulfilled a mission for this time.

Greg was an effective and inspiring preacher of the gospel. He had great "style" as well as excellent content, and the men responded. Like many of us, he filed an appeal based on some great arguments. However, most of became accustomed to being denied by the courts. It was very apparent to most of us there was no justice available in our current judicial environment.

The time came for him to leave, and I deferred my speaking times to him. For that final chapel, the place was packed to capacity. Kerry sang Ray Bolt's song, "Thank You" as a fitting tribute. Then the choir did some a capella numbers. Greg took time to tell the guys what a gracious co-worker I had been and that our relationship had always been harmonious. Then he preached his farewell sermon and it was terrific.

Late that evening he spent the time making his rounds to say goodbye. He passed out business cards in hopes many would connect on the outside. He also gave me his personal unlisted home phone number.

The following morning, he left. His wife was there to pick him up. There were many carloads of well-wishers who had driven from Birmingham to accompany him home. There were also busloads present rejoicing that this part of the judgment was over. The major networks were there and Greg was interviewed. Even an Alabama news helicopter was there filming the whole thing. It will be interesting to see if Greg can make political waves now that he is back home.

Santita Delaney

To Pastor/Friend Bob Bedford,

When I sit and observe Pastor Bob, in essence, I think of the Apostle Paul. A man who was very knowledgeable of the Word of God. A man full of wisdom, full of the fruits and gifts of the Holy Spirit. Full of revelations. A man who shared and instructed the Word of God even in prison. A man who rejoiced in the Lord in spite of his imprisonment. A man who not only preached and taught the Word of God but helped raise up young ministers like Timothy and Titus.

A man who has faith and everyday sowed that faith in his talk as well as his walk. A man who instructed churches to fight the good fight of faith. And also advised them to always study the word of God. Nevertheless, Paul said in 1 Corinthians 11:1 to follow him as he followed Christ, so is this with me toward Pastor Bob. Also, if it was not for Pastor Bob I would be a step behind, but with him, he has equipped me to move forward into what God has called me to do for His Kingdom. I most definitely thank God for Pastor Bob. My prayer is that God will keep him in good health and hive him long life because as Pastor Bob lives, he will continue to be about his Father's (God's) business.

--From Bro Santita Delaney

Santita is now working and pastoring in Mississippi.

Judge Teel

I mentioned earlier about a judge who came and then quickly had a heart attack. He had been accused of bribery. He was also tried twice and the federal judge in his case was also a man of injustice. The case in which he supposedly was bribed was a civil case that settled without trial so he could not have influenced the case. The judge would not even give the jury the instructions in writing. He was sentenced to 7.5 years and the judge refused an appeal bond.

I was thrilled when later the Appeals Court threw out 4 of the 5 convictions. While the fifth one should have been dismissed as well, it resulted in a significantly less sentence.

I noted on February 2008, that I felt moved to go see Wes, and I ministered to him for about 30 minutes. We prayed together for his wife, Myrna, who has MS and is rarely able to come visit him. When I told him we would put out a prayer request on our network, he wept and thanked me for giving him a "pastoral visit."

Later, he gave me an article that explained his case. It appears he got railroaded as badly as I did. He also very aware that appeals rarely work in the present judicial environment.

Wes also expressed to me that he could be grateful for the prison experience because it had forced him to move from a nominal Christian to a dynamic relationship with Christ.

Wes and Myrna now live in Oxford MS where their granddaughter attends the University of Mississippi.

On Special Assignment

Dr Steve

Steve arrived at the camp on 1/3/2008. I was coming into the dorm when Pastor Lee introduced me to him. It was obvious that he was bewildered by being thrust into a strange place. Lee went to get him a Christian care package (basic supplies such as soap, toothpaste, toothbrush, comb, shower shoes, etc.) While he was retrieving that I took Steve to my cube to inform him of the unwritten (but you're expected to know) rules.

Almost immediately Steve began to give me his story. Reared in a Jewish home in New York, he had come to the Atlanta area to pursue setting up a podiatry practice some years prior. (Steve was then 46.) He'd had many female relationships through the years but had never married. Both his parents had deceased. He had one sister who was a pediatrician with a practice in New York.

Steve told me about his practice and other businesses that he had had. Problems had developed that caused him to lose it all. Prior to his surrendering to custody, he lost his home and all other possessions. Other than one friend, whom he had unselfishly helped, all his other "friends" disowned him as soon as he was arrested. So Steve cam with a profound sense of loss and loneliness.

Steve did not tell me on that first night anything about his personal spiritual beliefs and I did not ask. My purpose that first day was to demonstrate the true love of God for which there is no expectation. For the first ten days or so after his arrival, Steve would op over to my cube to get more info or to simply talk.

Elsewhere on the compound, Steve met Dr Mike who also engaged him in conversation, and invited him to start attending the afternoon Bible study held in his cube each afternoon. We were pleasantly surprised when he started coming. After a few days we learned he had been reared as a Conservative Jew. We discovered that he had no Bible and, in fact, had never seen, much less read, the New Testament.

Since Mike had recently acquired a new Bible, he gave his old one to Steve, and asked him to read the four gospels which he gladly agreed to do. He was also given the book, "The Case for Faith" by Lee Strobel. Mike regularly engage Steve in conversation and explained the basics of Christianity. We began to pray in earnest for Steve's salvation.

Steve continued to attend Bible study and come by my room for conversation. Mike would frequently engage him in kingdom conversation. Mike reported to me on several occasions that God was working in Steve's life and he believed he would soon accept Jesus Christ.

As I was leaving the dining hall at supper time, I noticed Mike and Steve in intense discussion. About a half hour later, both of them came to my cubicle. Steven had two more questions he needed answered. First, did he have to renounce his Jewish heritage before he could accept Christ. I told him that Judaism was the foundation of Christianity. Jesus Christ was the promised Messiah. In accepting Christ, he could still honor his Jewish heritage.

His second question was that he wondered how he could become good enough for Jesus to accept him. Of course, it was a pleasure to assure him that the gospel was that no one was acceptable in his own right, but Christ made us accepted when we acknowledged His atonement for us. (Eph 1:6) Then grace would begin to make us more like Christ.

Without hesitation, Steve responded, "Then I'm ready to accept Jesus as my Messiah." He explained how that as he read the Gospels that we was amazed at how clear the instructions were on how to live. He said Judaism had never done that for him. We then asked if he would like to be baptized and we schedule it. Meanwhile, Steve continued to read and study the New Testament and he grew significantly in the Lord over the next ten days.

On Saturday, Feb 9th, at 6 pm in E dorm, we assembled in my cubicle for another baptism. The candidate sat in the center surround by seven other men. Larry Roundtree opened with prayer. The previous convert baptized, Raymond began the scripture reading from Isaiah 53. Dr Ben finished reading that chapter. Dr Mike read from the Gospel of Matthew 4:12-17. Then Gary finished the reading from Romans 6;3-8.

I then gave the questions to Steve who answered with assurance. Following his responses, I prayed a dedicatory prayer and baptized

On Special Assignment

him in the name of the Father, Son, and Holy Spirit. The sweet presence of God settled in that cubicle and sealed the service.

I closed with giving Steve two blessings—one from the Old Testament (Num 6;24-26) and one from the New Testament (Jude 24-25). We praised God for another Jew being "completed" in Christ and we extended him the right hand of fellowship into the body of Christ.

By the end of February, Steve felt confident enough to lead in public prayer in our Bible study group. We all rejoiced at progress in living the Christian life. Especially in here, phonies are quickly identified. Those who lives are radically transformed are affirmed by most.

Steve declared no religious preference when he entered the camp. Later he decided to order some of the Jewish Passover items so he turned in an order. It was rejected because they said he was "protestant." And he couldn't change his preference until next year. He then signed up for the Christian special meal for Pentecost Sunday only to be rejected because he's Jewish! ACD x 2! It was great that Steve could laugh at it.

Steve became steadfast in reading the scripture and witnessing to his newfound faith. He even told the rabbi that he was now a Messianic Jew. One clear evidence of his radical transformation was displayed in an act of kindness. A fellow by the name Andrea was very ill, but the officer was insisting that he do his work assignment anyway. As soon as Steve heard what was happening, he went to the officer and told him that he had to go do his own work assignment in the kitchen but as soon as he was through, he would come back and do whatever work was assigned to Andrea.

The officer was baffled and wanted to know why he would do that. He suspected that perhaps Steve was indebted to Andreas and that he was paying a debt. But other than greeting him in passing, they had not established any relationship. When Steve explained, he would simply do this as an act of love to a needy human being, and the officer saw he was sincere, it allowed Steve to tell him that the doctor had already given Andreas a convalescence pass. Andreas had been so muddled in his thinking he had failed to mention it. So the officer went and verified the doctor had written the pass and the matter was dropped.

Steve's cheerful willingness to go the "second mile" as a sheer act of love had been clearly demonstrated by someone who six months prior had never read or heard any of the teaching of Jesus. To whom do you show practical love? To those you know and love you? "For if you love those who love you, what reward have you." (Matthew 5:46) Christians too seldom act like Christ. The power and authority of the Kingdom only comes by obedient living to the commands of Christ. People will be drawn to Christ, not just by hearing the gospel, but seeing it lived out sincerely and cheerfully.

Steve applied for the drug program although he had never been a user. It was granted and he received notice he was to be transferred to Texarkana. He was "packed out" and sent to the holding unit to fly to the transfer facility in Oklahoma City. He expressed his sadness at leaving because he was leaving the best friends he had ever had in his entire life.

Anthony

Anthony grew up in the typical dysfunction of so many American families. His parents were part of the drug culture. They divorced when he was young and both have had multiple marriages.

With no moral compass, it was easy for Anthony to follow in his father's footsteps and he and his sister became drug users at an early age. He was branded with multiple tattoos, the status symbol of our declining culture.

The drug use and distribution eventually landed him in prison. He spent several months in a detention facility before being transferred to a federal camp.

Meanwhile, God had intervened in Anthony's father's life and he was thoroughly converted. He entered full-time ministry working with the down and out. He began praying for his son.

God placed Anthony in this dorm in the rear right next to the spot where the prayer circle met each evening. One night he was on the phone with his sister who is still a drug addict and alcoholic. When he finished that conversation just after the prayer time had ended, he came over to Lee and me and asked that we would pray for his sister, even though he was not a believer.

The following day his sister reported a drug-free day, a direct answer to prayer. The following night Anthony joined the prayer circle, which was a Friday night, Good Friday. One Easter Sunday, he and his friend Sidney came forward in the chapel service and were gloriously converted.

Changing old habits is never easy, but it continued to happen. Enrolling in the discipleship class taught by Lee, he memorized several verses of scripture.

The next step was baptism and we set it for the next Sunday night at the same altar at which he was converted. Sidney joined him, and Paul also came for baptism. As was our practice, we asked them the questions we pose to all candidates. The candidates all answered in a loud and affirming voice.

They knelt and prayer was offered and the familiar words, "I baptize you in the name of the Father, Son, and Holy Ghost" were spoken as the water was poured. The benediction of Hebrews 13:20-21 was given and the men rose to receive the "right hand of fellowship." He was also given his baptismal certificate to commemorate that day.

Two weeks later I met Anthony's father in the visiting room and we shared a moment of rejoicing with the angels that another "sinner had come home." Anthony joined our nightly prayer circle, and on May 15, he led in a public prayer for the first time in his life.

Linda's Thanksgiving Message in 2008

(This was written at Thanksgiving time. I had served sixteen months at the time. Three and a half months earlier Linda had fallen and shattered her left femur into eight major pieces. The orthopedist had repaired her with a titanium plate and many screws, plus bone grafts. She was not fully rehabilitated when this was written and she was just beginning to place weight on her leg.)

In Thanksgiving!

November 26, 2008 at 2:55pm

We have much for which to be thankful! Some may look at us and say, "How can they be thankful when they are going through difficult circumstances?" My answer is, "It's easy! Just look at what others have gone through this year such as those who have lost loved ones in death. Or other tragic events in their lives." Bob and I have each other -- we have a wonderful family who is unbelievably supportive. We have time together -- no, not every day as most of you have but when we are together, we have little to none of the distractions which are common in everyday life -- no TV, no phone, no cell phones ringing, no computers, no interruptions by text messaging, etc. Just time together! We have telephone calls each evening and I can guarantee you that you can say a whole lot more than you think you can in 15 minutes. Yes, I make lists sometimes -- other times, Bob has lots to share of what has happened in his day. I realized that when we were together all the time, we had a tendency to take each other for granted. We could always talk -- really talk -- sometime -- but not necessarily right then. Now, we do talk about important things -- intentionally!

We are thankful for how our ministry has grown -- from Bob's ministry there to our ministry through the devotionals, etc. When we hear how one of the devotionals has impacted someone's life, we know we are indeed blessed! When Bob sees the guys he is mentoring / ministering to growing spiritually, we are again so grateful for what God is doing in our lives. Remember -- it's all in the perspective.

On Special Assignment

The Bible tells us to give thanks "in" all things. Are we always thankful "for" things ... well, no, not always. But, we know that He works everything for our good and so far that, we can "in everything" give thanks.

Some things I am thankful for:

1. For a husband who loves God and spends time in His Word daily! For his daily calls and letters which reaffirm our love and commitment to each other. For the time we have together when I visit - completely devoted to one another without the typical distractions of computer, cell phones, TV, etc.

2. For four wonderful daughters, Roxanne, Sandi, Teri and Shonna, who have all chosen to serve Christ. They are not only my daughters but truly my best friends. For their willingness to do whatever is needed - especially over the past months since the surgery on my leg. I owe them a huge debt of gratitude for their constant care!

3. For their support in all ways - from physical care to emotional support. They have been willing to listen when I was rather 'down' and have kept me focused on what was important.

4. For four sons-in-law, Chris, Tim, Jeff and Ron, who treat me well - I've heard the horror stories about mothers-in-law and hope they do not consider me one of those 'horrible' ones.

5. For four of the most beautiful granddaughters in the whole world, Kasi, Marley, Regan and Bailey - of course, every grandmother says that! And we would expect that! But, I still think mine are the best!

6. For four of the most handsome grandsons in the whole world, Kamen, Tyler, RJ and Rudy, who aren't embarrassed to give Nana a hug in front of everyone!

7. For one sweet new great-granddaughter, Ava, who has already wrapped her little fingers around our hearts.
8. For wonderful families - from my dad who calls me almost daily

just to 'check in' to my siblings; my sister, Rachel, who is also my closest friend, and her husband, Allen; my brothers, Tim & his wife, Susan, Mark & his wife, Shelley, Joel and Thad. I could not ask for a more supportive family! Many of my trips to Atlanta are spent on the phone with one or more of the siblings along the way - again, just 'checking in'. Of course, the fact that I am the oldest and some refer to me as the 'matriarch' since my mother's passing keeps me even more connected! (I'm not sure whether 'matriarch' makes me feel older or not!)

9. For not just my family but Bob's family who is right there with us - his mother, Nell Bedford, who is of great support; his brother, Bill and his wife, Barb, and his sisters, Betty & Gene, Linda & Tom, and Nancy. I don't ever feel like an "in-law" when I am with them - just part of the family and for that I am blessed.

10. For friends - we are so very blessed with such a wonderful group of friends. From all over the United States and even in foreign countries, we are so honored! We are so blessed by notes of encouragement!

11. For new found friends - when we entered this part of our lives, we had no idea the number of new friends we would make nor how close those friendships would develop. It's rare that I don't hear by email from some of them daily and I know I can pick up the phone and call one at any time!

12. For God providing for our needs. I am constantly amazed at how God provides just when we need it.

13. For God's protection as we travel. Just this week, we drove to Atlanta and back. The next morning, we realized there was a problem with the van. The mechanic was very surprised we had not had a problem on the way home and I knew it was God's protection. (I wasn't necessarily thankful for the repair bill!)

14. For humor in our lives - one of the trademarks of our families has been humor and that can usually be found in our 'silly photos' which it seems we cannot live without! No matter how serious the occasion (even at my mother's funeral), during any family photos, you will hear someone yell (literally), "Silly photo. 1-2-3!" I know - sort of crazy, isn't it? Perhaps it is what helps us keep our sanity!!

15. For the many notes - emails and snail mail we have received over the past 16+ months. We cannot begin to express our appreciation for these! Each evening, Bob tells me about the mail he receives. He has sent large packages of mail back to me and someday, we hope to put those into a scrapbook. Especially the postcards from across the United States sent from Rollin Mitchell and others who write Bob on a regular basis.

God's Character School—Life Lessons Taught

Everything that happens in our life is for our benefit. We are not always in the learning mode, but we should be. The Holy Spirit is our teacher, and he is always available for every teaching moment. While this list will not be exhaustive, it will be significant because of the time spent in meditation before, during, and after my confinement. These are placed in a specific order, and they are all important.

1. When God has a special assignment, he always looks for a person (man/woman) and not a committee, group, or institution. There are biblical examples such as Noah, Moses, Daniel, and many others. His criteria are not revealed to us, but we know that he looks to one he can trust and that he can prepare.

2. God's methodology always defies conventional wisdom. He does a character examination and often we are perplexed. For example, who would choose a fugitive murderer to lead the Exodus? And God had to even convince Moses via a meaningful dialogue.

3. God's preparation for major assignments is never predicated on time. He will use hours, days, or year. For Joseph, it was about 14 years; for Moses, it was 40 years; for Noah, it was 120 years. God often used the prophets on the "spur of the moment" even though they had personally allowed God to prepare them ahead of time.

4. God's assignment is always bigger than human effort can accomplish. If you can envision how you will achieve the assignment, then it's not God's vision. For "without faith, it is impossible to please God." (Hebrews 11:6)

5. The grace to empower us to accomplish God's assignment is received by humility. "God resists the proud, but gives grace to the humble." (James 4:6) If you wish to double your reception of grace, then do accept the humbling situation with cheerfulness. (See 2 Corinthians 9:7-8)

6. God's work always requires complete trust, abiding faith, and accepting mystery. God allows life circumstances that remove all the props with which we have surrounded

ourselves. He knocks out our self-reliance until trusting God is the only thing we can do. We use the phrase "living by faith" but it terrifies us to do it. We can't just start with faith, it must continue through all difficulties. We have a hard time letting God be God—we want him to explain all the details. He doesn't need our two cents, but he will mightily use us if we'll only let God have his full control of our lives.

7. **God's work is always the redemption of individuals and society.** "O perfect redemption, the purchase of blood, To every believer the promise of God; The vilest offender who truly believes, That moment from Jesus a pardon receives." From the song, To God Be the Glory." No matter where our assignment takes us, our mission is always redemption.

8. God allows negative experiences in our lives—He has a purpose even though it is hidden from us. 2 Cor 1:7, "We are confident that as you share in our sufferings, you will also share in the comfort God gives us." (Holy Bible, New Living Translation ®, copyright © 1996, 2004 by Tyndale Charitable Trust. Used by permission of Tyndale House Publishers. All rights reserved.)

9. God uses every circumstance for His glory and our good. See Romans 8:28. It is often very difficult to see what God's purpose is while we are undergoing the processes. We may wander searching for meaning and purpose, but God is always on track.

10. Suffering produces faithfulness when embraced with joy. The old expression "no pain, no gain" applies to our Christian life. Those who believe the believer's life can be lived without suffering, have missed the scripture and the example of Jesus. Suffering strips us of ungodly desires. It forces us to narrow our thinking to essential matters. Illicit desires give way to purposeful ones. Paul reminds us that "all who live godly will suffer persecution." (2 Tim 3:12) The essential qualification to get named in the Hall of Faith (Hebrews 11) was having endured suffering. See 1 Thess 1:6, Hebrews 12:2, James 1:2.

11. God rarely answer our prayers in the way we expect—but He does answer. Someone said, "God answers with a no, yes, or I've got a better idea." We must always resist the temptation to box God into answering the way we want. Our small mind-set causes us to not recognize when God is actually working.

12. When circumstances are beyond our control, God is still in control. He instructs us many times about the difference between our way of thinking versus His. (Isa 55:9 NASU) "For as the heavens are higher than the earth, So are My ways higher than your ways And My thoughts than your thoughts." Paul adds to this, (Eph 3:20 NASU), "Now to Him who is able to do far more abundantly beyond all that we ask or think, according to the power that works within us." See also Philippians 3:21.

13. Our call (mission, assignment) does not change because our venue does. God is not at work in just one place or time. He is always engaged in the mission (the Great Commission.)

EPILOGUE

I am always amazed at the work God is doing in the world. God works in foreign lands, often amidst tremendous persecution. But God is also at work in the prisons in America. Many men find God and discover that He had been looking for them all along. They were just too distracted to notice "the hound of heaven" on their trail.

We often wonder why God allowed difficult issues to come into our lives. He always has a plan—we're just not clued in at the time. Such questions came to my mind, and it was something with which I wrestled frequently. From day one in confinement, God kept me on track.

The summary of things that God accomplished while I was there are:

1. There were 66 men who made a first-time commitment to serve Jesus. We were able to baptize over 50 of those men

2. Our friends, the Stimacks, joined in ministry to place leather-bound, name inscribed study bibles to 75 men who agreed to read and study daily and to start a bible study group in their respective dorms.

3. There were 75 bible study groups organized and each attracted 5-10 men—most were daily times.

4. Over 200 men were involved in those daily studies. The key focus of the groups was not just to increase the bible knowledge, but the focus was on living out the gospel on a daily basis. It involved accountability for actions and attitudes; it's what I call genuine discipleship.

5. A Bible School was established in which 15 men were enrolled. Several completed the course of study. Because I was given the responsibility to manage the chapel, all those who wished to do so were given the opportunity to preach, and thereby improve their skills where they could receive constructive criticism.

6. Two men were ordained. One who remained at the facility accepted responsibility to continue the ministry and did so for almost seven more years, getting released in January 2017. The other one now lives close and is my partner in many ministry assignments.

On Special Assignment

7. There have been over 80 additional bibles placed since my release in May 2010, each creating another bible study group.

8. There have been over 70 additional conversions, and over 50 baptisms.

If any of you are familiar with "recidivism" you would know that the national statistic is that nearly 70% of those released from prison will return to prison within three years of release.

Here are the numbers from the Bureau of Justice.

- 67.5% of prisoners released in 1994 were rearrested within 3 years, an increase over the 62.5% found for those released in 1983

- The re-arrest rate for property offenders, drug offenders, and public-order offenders increased significantly from 1983 to 1994. During that time, the re-arrest rate increased:

- from 68.1% to 73.8% for property offenders

- from 50.4% to 66.7% for drug offenders

- from 54.6% to 62.2% for public-order offenders

- The re-arrest rate for violent offenders remained relatively stable (59.6% in 1983 compared to 61.7% in 1994).

Prisons have little to no effective programs to turn men away from evil. There is some education available but changing hearts is not the focus. The odds are stacked against one being released. Often, they are without marketable skills, and obtaining a job is difficult at best. Finding housing and transportation is also a major challenge. If they have been incarcerated long term (ten years or more) the world has changed substantially. Many return to crime as their way to survive.

I have remained in contact with about 50 men from Atlanta, and their circles reach out to a total of over 200 men. Of that group, the recidivism rate is ZERO. Total life change was the goal of our discipleship program and God answered that prayer. To Him be all the glory!

Ten of the men enrolled in the bible school are currently serving in ministry capacities—pastor, associate pastor, and evangelist. Several were able to plant new churches.

God provided the grace to live victoriously while there, and that grace was shared to the many men with whom I lived. Of course, I would never wish to re-live those days, but God has been faithful. My desire is that this story would encourage you in whatever challenge you are in. God has an ultimate purpose even if you don't currently understand what that is. It is a matter of complete trust! Accept your mission!

--Bob Bedford

www.ingramcontent.com/pod-product-compliance
Lightning Source LLC
Chambersburg PA
CBHW061648040426
42446CB00010B/1647